craft **workshop**

wire

craft **workshop**

wire

The art of decorating with wire in 25 beautiful projects

Mary Maguire

photography by Peter Williams

southwater

For my father

THIS EDITION IS PUBLISHED BY SOUTHWATER

DISTRIBUTED IN THE UK BY
THE MANNING PARTNERSHIP
251–253 LONDON ROAD EAST
BATHEASTON, BATH BA1 7RL
TEL. 01225 852 727
FAX 01225 852 852

PUBLISHED IN THE USA BY
ANNESS PUBLISHING INC.
27 WEST 20TH STREET
SUITE 504, NEW YORK NY 10011
FAX 212 807 6813

DISTRIBUTED IN CANADA BY
GENERAL PUBLISHING
895 DON MILLS ROAD
400–402 PARK CENTRE
TORONTO, ONTARIO M3C 1W3
TEL. 416 445 3333
FAX 416 445 5991

DISTRIBUTED IN AUSTRALIA BY
SANDSTONE PUBLISHING
UNIT 1, 360 NORTON STREET
LEICHHARDT, NEW SOUTH WALES 2040
TEL. 02 9560 7888
FAX 02 9560 7488

SOUTHWATER IS AN IMPRINT OF
ANNESS PUBLISHING LIMITED
HERMES HOUSE, 88–89 BLACKFRIARS ROAD
LONDON SE1 8HA
TEL. 020 7401 2077; FAX 020 7633 9499

PUBLISHER: JOANNA LORENZ
SENIOR EDITOR: CLARE NICHOLSON
PHOTOGRAPHER: PETER WILLIAMS
DESIGNER: PETER BUTLER
STYLIST: GEORGINA RHODES
ILLUSTRATOR: VANA HAGGERTY

PREVIOUSLY PUBLISHED AS *NEW CRAFTS: WIREWORK*

10 9 8 7 6 5 4 3 2 1

PUBLISHER'S NOTE
WORKING WITH WIRE IS GREAT FUN AND CAN FILL MANY
REWARDING HOURS. FOR SAFETY, PROTECTIVE GLOVES
SHOULD BE WORN WHEN USING WIRE THAT HAS SHARP
ENDS, SUCH AS CHICKEN WIRE.

CONTENTS

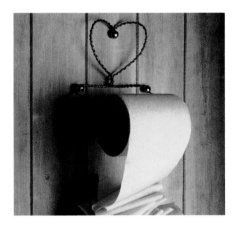

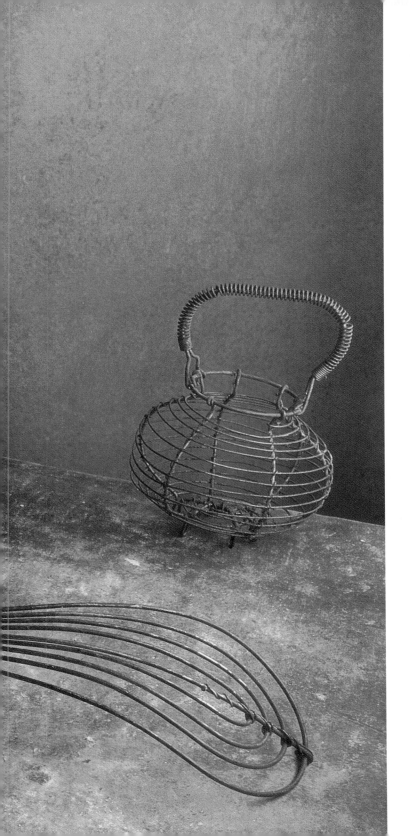

INTRODUCTION

T HE CRAFT OF WIREWORK HAS BEEN SADLY NEGLECTED IN RECENT YEARS BUT IS NOW MAKING A COMEBACK, AND WIRE CREATIONS CAN BE SEEN IN FASHIONABLE SHOPS, MAGAZINES AND GALLERIES. WIRE IS AN AMAZINGLY VERSATILE MATERIAL REQUIRING FEW TOOLS TO MANIPULATE IT, BESIDE YOUR HANDS. THE BOOK WILL ENABLE YOU TO MAKE YOUR OWN WIREWORK CREATIONS BY FOLLOWING THE STEP-BY-STEP INSTRUCTIONS FOR EACH PROJECT. THE BASIC TECHNIQUES SECTION EXPLAINS THE DIFFERENT WAYS OF MANIPULATING AND SHAPING WIRE USED IN THE PROJECTS. THE GALLERY SHOWS A RANGE OF WIRE STRUCTURES MADE BY ARTISTS, AND AIMS TO INSPIRE YOU TO DEVELOP WORKS OF YOUR OWN DESIGN.

Opposite: These whisks and baskets are typical examples of the wirework items being produced in Britain and France at the turn of the twentieth century. With the renewed interest in wirework, there are many reproductions of such kitchen implements available today.

HISTORY OF WIRE

WIREWORK IS AN ANCIENT ART FORM, PROBABLY FIRST PRACTISED BY THE EGYPTIANS AROUND 3000 BC. EARLY EXAMPLES HAVE BEEN DISCOVERED IN THE BURIAL CHAMBERS OF IMPORTANT PEOPLE THROUGHOUT THE ANCIENT WORLD. IN 2600 BC, WIRE WAS USED IN GOLD AND SILVER RIBBONS FOR ENTWINING IN THE HAIR OF COURTLY LADIES IN THE SUMERIAN CITY OF UR. THE ART OF WIREWORK SPREAD IN VARIOUS FORMS FROM BABYLON TO BAGHDAD, DAMASCUS AND CONSTANTINOPLE BEFORE FINALLY REACHING EUROPE.

Wire was originally made by chiselling thin strips from a sheet of metal. The strips were either twisted and then rolled between two flat surfaces to smooth them or spirally wound around a mandrel.

Today wire is made by drawing rods of metal through conically shaped holes in a draw-plate. This system was first used in Persia in the sixth century BC but did not reach Europe until the tenth century AD when wire was first being produced on a commercial scale. The iron wire trade made chain-mail, and also wool carders, girdles, chains, fish hooks and needles. Up until this time gold and silver wires were made almost exclusively for jewellery but during the Middle Ages embroidery became their principal use. In England, the two trades were governed by different bodies, the Broiders' Company and the Girdler and Pinmakers' Company. It was not until the late seventeenth century that they became distinctive guilds known as the Worshipful Company of Gold and Silver Wireworkers', and the Worshipful Company of Tin Plates alias Wireworkers.

By the mid-sixteenth century, there were at least 6000 wire drawers in London alone and it was around this time that the first mechanical drawing machines were used in England. The water-driven draw-plate system used in these machines was invented by Rudolf of Nuremberg in the fourteenth century, but was not introduced to England until 1564. Gold and silver wirework flourished

until the time of the French Revolution when fashions changed and the industry went into decline.

Because of the corrodible nature of iron, very few examples of the broad range of objects once made from iron wire have survived to this day, save the items mentioned above and a few toys and

Above: These two pieces of wirework were made in Mexico. The enchanting giraffe design doubles up as a basket. The wire cupboard stands approximately 60 cm (2 ft) high.

Left: This motorcycle and Volkswagen car were made in Zimbabwe.

Below: These horses were made by apprentice wireworkers in Zimbabwe. The horses are made from recycled flip flops.

Bottom: The levers and cables on this piece are fully operational.

traps. By the early nineteenth century, tinning and black-japanning had become popular ways of protecting the wireworker's craft. Not only did these treatments prevent rusting, they also helped cement items made from unsoldered wire.

America imported its wire from England and Germany until 1812, when the war with England meant that supplies were cut off. From this point, the Americans started building their own factories for producing wire. By the mid-nineteenth century, the steam engine enabled wire, woven wire and wire fencing to be mass produced. The industry flourished, reaching its peak in Europe and America at the turn of the century, when an impressive range of products was available from wire whisks and baskets to wire gazebos. The craft of wireworking was applied to every possible household device until the advent of plastic gradually led to its demise.

Wirework is still alive and well in many countries around the world, as shown by the examples from Africa and Mexico. In Europe, with the renewed interest in folk art, the craft is enjoying a renaissance.

GALLERY

IN THE 1920S, THE AMERICAN ARTIST ALEXANDER CALDER BROUGHT WIRE INTO PROMINENCE IN THE WORLD OF FINE ART WITH HIS WIRE SCULPTURES AND DRAWINGS OF PEOPLE AND ANIMALS, WHICH ARE AS FRESH AND ALIVE TODAY AS THEY WERE THEN. TODAY THERE ARE MANY ARTISTS WORKING IN WIRE. THE GALLERY ILLUSTRATES A BROAD CROSS-SECTION OF CONTEMPORARY WIREWORK USES AND TECHNIQUES.

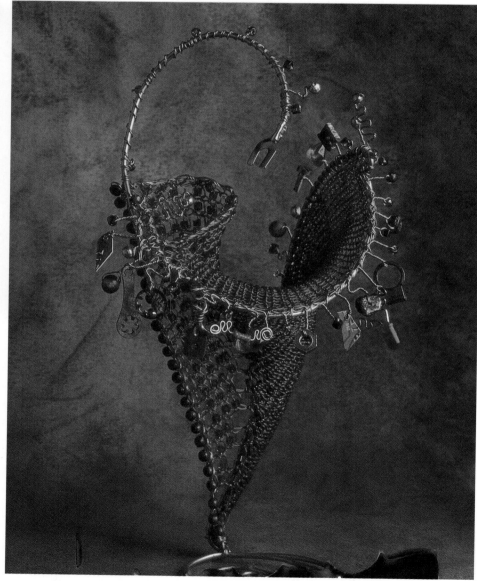

Above: CANDLE HOLDERS
The lantern, candle holder and candle stick have all been made from small-gauge chicken wire. The base of the candle holder has been crafted from wire mesh spoons which are available from oriental shops. Chicken wire makes beautifully light candle holders which are safe to use inside as well as outside.
CLARE NICHOLSON

Right: VENUS
This standing sculpture, which measures 18 x 9 cm (7 x 3½ in), was knitted in coloured enamelled fuse wire around a copper wire frame. Objects such as electrical components and glass beads add to the rich texture of the piece.
JAN TRUMAN

Left: NOAH'S ARK
This wire sculpture, which is approximately 3.5 m (11 ft) long, is made from chased, rolled and etched copper and binding wire, then cast silver and bronze have been added. Several parts of the sculpture are made from recycled materials such as rusty beer cans.
CATHY PILKINGTON

Right: CROCHETED GLOVES
These elegant gloves are made of flat panels crocheted in 0.2 mm (0.008 in) silver wire which have been seamed together with gussets in the same way that leather gloves are made. French knots have been embroidered along the main gauntlet and hammered silver discs sewn on between the knots. The bobbles were made from a double thickness of crocheting. The gloves have been oxidized to give them their dark patina.
SUSAN CROSS

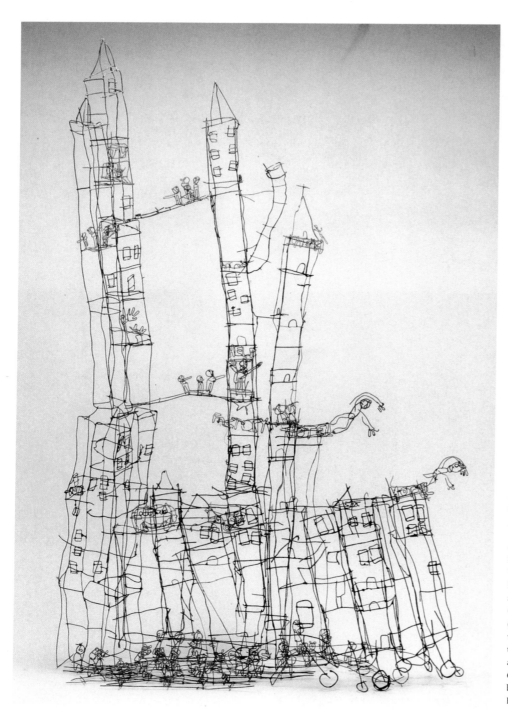

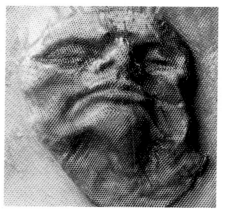

Above: TORTURED HEAD
The head was first drawn from life, then a piece of Perspex was placed over the drawing and a relief model built up around it in clay. A plaster mould was made of the clay model as a negative image, from which a second mould was made as a positive image. Aluminium mesh was compressed between the two moulds to take the form of the head and finally layers of aluminium were applied. It is 30 x 30 cm (12 x 12 in) in size.
JANE MACADAM-FREUD

Left: METROPOLIS
Inspired by a trip to Las Vegas, Metropolis is Paul's response to the alienation of urban life. Constructed from 1 m (1 yd) lengths of silver wire soldered together, the structure is approximately 90 x 60 cm (3 x 2 ft). It has been painted in places.
PAUL DAVIS

Opposite: WIRE-MESH GEESE
These sculpted life-size animals are caught in mid-action while exploring a kitchen. The malleability of wire lends itself well to sections such as the necks, which are stretched curiously into nooks and crannies. The geese are made from recycled rabbit netting which has been reclaimed from old pheasant-rearing pens.
RUPERT TILLS

Right: FRUIT FUNNEL
Hans makes
predominantly functional
food-related
constructions; this
beautifully undulating
funnel is designed to
gauge fruit according to
its size. The starkness of
its form and colour
contrasts with the bright
colours of the vegetables.
The funnel was made
from spot-welded mild
steel wire which was
then heat-blackened.
HANS STOFER

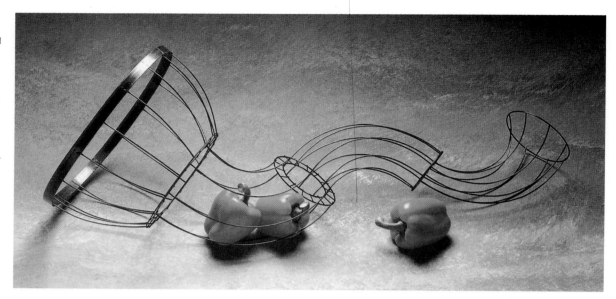

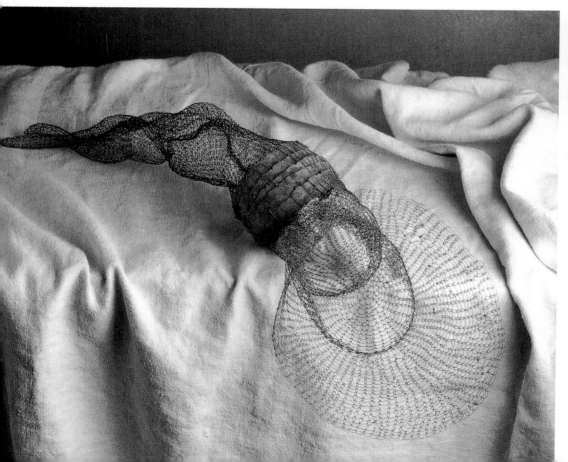

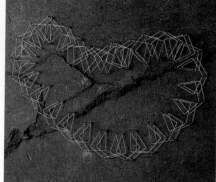

Left: DISCARDED SKIN
This wire sculpture,
measuring 65 cm (26 in)
in length, is made from a
section of etched and
coloured steel strips
which are held together
with woven soft wire.
Amanda Bright works
exclusively in steel with
soft wire and is inspired
by the material
properties of steel.
AMANDA BRIGHT

Above: NECK PIECE
This neck piece was
made from articulated
lengths of stainless steel
wire. Its success lies in
the simplicity of line and
the beautiful movement
within the piece when
handled or worn.
ESTER WARD

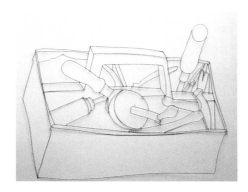

Above: TOOL BOX
Tony Eve uses wire as everybody else uses a pencil. He creates a simple wire outline to "draw" objects from tool boxes to bicycles. These structures have a charming wit and simplicity.
TONY EVE

Right: HAT AND SHOES
These pieces have been woven out of enamelled copper wire. The hat was inspired by ancient Greek helmets. The ornamentation on the shoes is attached through the laces.
ADELE TIPLER

Left: TREASURE BASKET
Drawing on her textile background and basket-making skills, Hillary has created a wirework basket approximately 15 x 20 cm (6 x 8 in) in size. A grid was drawn on a wooden former and panel pins were hammered in at the intersections. The structural wires were anchored to make them manageable, then short lengths of assorted wire were woven around the main struts and through metal and rubber washers and grommets. The ends of the wires were then looped around and wrapped.
HILLARY BURNS

MATERIALS

WIRE IS MADE BY DRAWING RODS OF METAL THROUGH CONICALLY SHAPED HOLES IN A DRAW-PLATE. ROUND WIRE IS THE MOST COMMON BUT SQUARE, HEXAGONAL AND HALF-ROUND WIRES ARE ALSO AVAILABLE. AS WELL AS MEASURING WIRE IN MILLIMETRES OR INCHES, GAUGES ARE ALSO USED IN WHICH THE MEASUREMENTS RANGE FROM 0 TO AROUND 50. THE SMALLER THE NUMBER, THE THICKER THE WIRE. DIFFERENT COUNTRIES HAVE DIFFERENT GAUGES. HOWEVER, THE MEASUREMENTS FOR WIRE IN THE PROJECTS ARE GIVEN IN MILLIMETRES AND INCHES.

Enamelled copper wire is primarily used in the electronics industry but is ideal for wirework because of the wide range of colours. Available from some craft and electrical shops but, for the full range of colours and gauges, by mail order from suppliers. It also comes on industrial-sized spools for the real enthusiast.

Wire coat-hangers are cheap and widely available. They come in different finishes.

Tinned copper wire is shiny and does not tarnish, so it is particularly suitable

KEY
1, 2, 4, 5, 7, 11, 14, 15 Enamelled copper wire
3 Coat-hanger
6, 8, 9, 20, 23 Tinned copper wire
10, 26 Aluminium wire
12 Twisty wire tape
19, 21 Garden wire
16, 18, 24, 28 Copper wire
17, 25, 27 Straining wire
13, 22 Galvanized wire

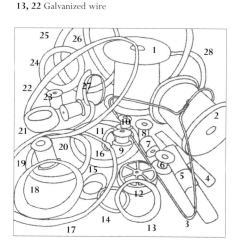

for kitchenware. Available by mail order from suppliers in a broad range of gauges.

Aluminium wire is a dull blue-grey colour. Of all the wires listed, it is the easiest to work with because it is so soft and easy to bend. Available by mail order from suppliers.

Garden wire is easy to manipulate and kind to the hands as it is plastic-coated. It comes in various shades of green and in different thicknesses. It is perfect for crafting bathroom or kitchen accessories because it is waterproof, hardwearing and colourful. Available from hardware stores and gardening shops.

Copper wire has an attractive, warm colour and can be bought in different tempers (hardnesses). Soft copper wire is easy to work with and has been used for the projects in the book. Available in a broad range of gauges from some hardware stores and craft shops or by mail order from suppliers.

Straining wire is made up of thin strands of galvanized wire that have been twisted together, which gives this wire a nice texture and makes it very strong. As the wire is hard, caution needs to be taken when working with it. Available from hardware stores.

Galvanized wire is zinc-coated steel wire. The zinc coating prevents rusting, making this wire ideal for outdoor use. Galvanized wire is a hard wire, so it does not bend as easily as some of the other wire, and, because it is springy, caution needs to be taken when working with it. Available in approximately five gauges from hardware stores.

Chicken wire is made from galvanized steel wire. Usually used for fencing and animal pens, it comes with different-sized holes and in various widths. For the purposes of the projects in the book, we have used the smallest gauge. Chicken wire is a versatile craft material as it is

easy to manipulate and inexpensive. Available from hardware stores.

Silver-plated copper wire comes in small coils in many different gauges and is particularly suited to jewellery making and small, fine wirework. Available from jewellery craft shops.

Twisty wire tape is a thin, flat tape with a hidden wire core. It comes in various shades of green for gardening purposes and in blue and white for household usage. Strips of multicoloured freezer bag ties can also be bought. This material is not usually associated with crafts but it is a pleasing wire to work with and can be used by children if they are supervised. Available from gardening shops and supermarkets.

Above: Pipe cleaners and paper clips are less obvious wirework materials, but being inexpensive and coming in a variety of colours, shapes and sizes, they are great fun to work with. There are also many ways to decorate wire structures such as colouring wire with car spray paint as in the Seashore Mobile project, or using beads to embellish wire frames such as the Lantern project.

EQUIPMENT

ONLY THE MOST BASIC KINDS OF WIRE CUTTERS AND PLIERS ARE NEEDED TO MAKE THE PROJECTS IN THE BOOK. FOR SOME OF THE PROJECTS, YOU COULD GET AWAY WITH USING JUST ORDINARY GENERAL-PURPOSE PLIERS, ALTHOUGH THE MORE SPECIALIZED PLIERS MAKE SOME MODELLING JOBS MUCH EASIER. ROUND-NOSED PLIERS, WHICH ARE AVAILABLE FROM CRAFT SHOPS, ARE A WORTHWHILE INVESTMENT.

General-purpose pliers are the pliers that you are most likely to own already. They often have serrated jaws to give a strong grip. This can be a disadvantage in wirework as the serrations leave marks. Place a piece of leather between the pliers and the wire to prevent any marking.

Round-nosed pliers (also known as round-nosed jewellery pliers) are a good investment as they can be used for many different crafts as well as for mending broken jewellery. With these pliers, wire can be bent into tiny circles (see the Angel project). If you are planning to make many of the projects in the book it is worth investing in half-round pliers (also known as half-round jewellery pliers). These are useful for bending wire into broad curves (see the Seashore Mobile project). Both types are available from craft shops.

Wire cutters are extremely useful, even though the cutters on ordinary general-purpose pliers will do for most projects. Don't buy the smallest cutters available, as good leverage with long handles is needed when cutting galvanized wire.

Parallel pliers are useful because the jaws open and close parallel to each other, unlike ordinary pliers. Even when the jaws are smooth, they still grip well, as they hold along their full length rather than at just one point. For this reason they are suitable for straightening bent wire and bending angles.

Snipe-nosed pliers are useful for reaching into difficult places and are the best kind of pliers for working with chicken wire.

Hand drills are useful for twisting soft wires together (see Basic Techniques and the Fused Flowers project).

Wooden coat-hangers can be used for twisting galvanized wire together (see Basic Techniques and the Spice Rack project). Always make sure that the handle is securely attached and will not unscrew.

Permanent marker pens are essential for marking measurements on wire as felt-tips will just rub off.

Rolling pins and wooden spoons are two of many household items useful for making coils in wire (see Basic Techniques and the Hook Rack project). Keep your eye out for cylinders and pipes in varying sizes, which also might be useful for making coils.

Gardening gloves will protect your hands when working with chicken wire and other scratchy wire, such as straining wire. Wearing goggles is also advisable when manipulating long lengths of wire, especially if the wire is under tension as a loose end could whip up accidentally in your face. It is best to take precautions.

Ruler Many of the projects require accurate use of measurements. The measurements are given in both metric and imperial. It is essential to choose one set of measurements and to stick with it throughout each project to ensure accuracy.

Scissors are always an essential piece of equipment when working on craft projects. Sharp scissors will cut through thin wire but this is not advisable because it will blunt the blades.

Hammer A hammer is useful for flattening the ends of cut lengths of wire (see Toasting Fork project).

Block of wood When shaping wire (see Loo Roll Holder project) it is sometimes useful to use a gib which can be made with a screw and a piece of wood.

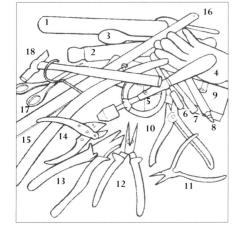

KEY
1, 2 Rolling pins
3 Wooden spoon
4 Gardening gloves
5 Hand drill
6, 7, 8 Permanent marker pens
9 Piece of wood
10 Wire cutters
11 Round-nosed pliers
12 Snipe-nosed pliers
13 General-purpose pliers
14 Parallel pliers
15 Wooden coat-hanger
16 Ruler
17 Scissors
18 Hammer

BASIC TECHNIQUES

WIRE IS A WONDERFULLY VERSATILE MATERIAL. IT CAN BE BRAIDED, CORDED, COILED, WRAPPED, TWISTED, WOVEN, CROCHETED, SPRUNG, SPIRALLED, FILIGREED AND FASHIONED INTO INNUMERABLE DIFFERENT SHAPES. OF THE MANY TECHNIQUES COMMONLY USED IN WIREWORK, INSTRUCTIONS ARE GIVEN HERE FOR THOSE USED TO MAKE THE PROJECTS IN THE BOOK. LOOK THROUGH THIS SECTION BEFORE STARTING ANY OF THE PROJECTS.

TWISTING WIRE

Twisting is a simple and effective way of joining two or more wires to add to their strength and texture.

Soft wires such as copper are the easiest to twist and using a hand drill speeds up the process. Harder wires such as galvanized wire require more effort and caution must be taken. Letting go of the wires prematurely may cause them to spin out of control which can be dangerous. If using a coat-hanger to twist the wires, choose the wooden type with a wire hook that revolves, ensuring that the handle is securely attached and will not unscrew.

Twisting Hard Wire

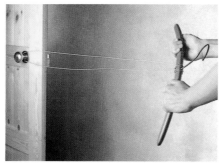

1 Cut a piece of wire at least three times as long as the required twisted length, depending on the degree of twist you want in the wire. Double the length of wire and loop it around a door handle or other suitably secure point. Wrap the loose ends very firmly three times around the hanger either side of the handle. Make sure that you hold the wire horizontally, otherwise you may get an uneven twist.

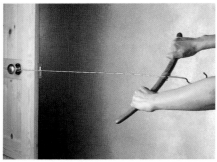

2 Brace yourself backwards to keep the wire taut and begin twisting the coat-hanger around. Do not relax your grip as this may cause an uneven texture.

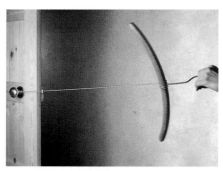

3 Twist the wire to the degree required, taking care not to overtwist as the wire may snap. To release the tension in the wire, hold the hanger firmly in one hand and grip its handle in the other. Quickly release your hold on the hanger, which will spin round a bit.

4 Remove the wire from the door handle and cut off the ends.

Twisting Soft Wire

1 Double the lengths of wire to be twisted. Two lengths have been used here. Loop the wires around a door handle and wrap the other ends with masking tape before securing them into the hand drill chuck.

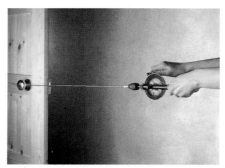

2 Keeping the wire taut, rotate the drill to twist the wire to the degree required. With soft wires there is no need to release the tension in the wire before removing from the drill bit and trimming.

WRAPPING WIRE

When wrapping wire, ideally the core wire should be thicker and harder than the wrapping wire, although two wires of the same thickness can be used as long as the wrapping wire is soft enough for the job. Copper wire is the most suitable. When cutting the core wire, remember to allow an excess of at least 6 cm (2½ in) to form the winding loop. The long lengths of soft wire used in wrapping can be unmanageable so if using long lengths coil the wire first, as described in method B.

1 Using round-nosed pliers, make a loop at the end of the core wire. Attach the wrapping wire to this loop.

2 Insert a pencil or other suitable object into the loop and use it as a winder. While winding, hold your thumb and index finger right up against the coil to ensure that the wire is closely wrapped.

Method B

1 Using round-nosed pliers, make a loop at the end of the core wire and bend the wire into a spiral along half its length. Form a loop at the other end of the core wire and secure the wrapping wire to the loop. Insert a pencil into the loop and use it as a winder.

2 Wrap a third of the wire, remove the pencil and coil the wire that has just been wrapped into a matching spiral. This section can now be used as the winder. Change the position of your hand so that it supports the core wire from beneath, with the wrapping wire running between your fingers and thumb.

Tips for Wrapping Wire

When using wire from a skein, keep it on the floor with your foot holding it in place. This will enable you to achieve the necessary tension for wrapping the wire.

When using wire from a spool, insert a long stick through it and hold it in place with your feet. This allows the spool to unwind quite freely while keeping the wire taut.

COILS

Coils are probably the most commonly used decorative device in wirework. They also have a practical use as they neaten and make safe what would otherwise be sharp ends, while adding grace and style.

Closed Coils

1 Using round-nosed pliers, make a small loop at the end of the wire.

2 Hold the loop firmly with parallel pliers. Use the pliers to bend the wire around until you have a coil of the size required. Keep adjusting the position of the pliers as you work.

Open Coils

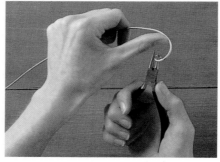

1 Using round-nosed pliers, make a small loop at the end of the wire. Holding the loop in the pliers, place your thumb against the wire and draw the wire across it to form a curve.

2 Use your eye to judge the space left between the rings of the coil.

3 Finally, carefully flatten the coil with parallel pliers.

Flattened Extended Coils

The flattened extended coil is a common structural and decorative device used in wirework. It is a quick and easy way to make the side walls of a container, for instance, and has been used to make the decorative trim at the front of the Spice Rack and the bracket at the back of the Hook Rack.

1 Wrap the wire several times around a broomstick or other cylindrical object to make a coil. If using galvanized wire, you will need to brace your thumb firmly against it.

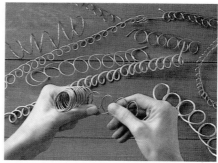

2 After removing the coil from the broomstick, splay out the loops one by one, holding them firmly between your fingers and thumbs.

3 Keep splaying out the loops until the whole coil has been flattened. The loops will now look more oval than round. You can stretch the coil further to open the loops if you wish.

WEAVING

Many basketwork and textile techniques can be applied to wirework, as illustrated in the gallery section by the woven hat and shoes and the crocheted jewellery. Knitting and lacemaking techniques can also be employed. Fine enamelled copper wire is especially suitable for weaving as it is soft and pliable and comes in a wide range of colours Of the techniques described here, methods B and C will give a more closely woven and tidier finish than method A. Method A is the simplest.

Method A

The quickest and easiest way to weave is to wind the wire in and out of the struts to create an open texture.

Method B

Weave around the struts by passing the wire over each strut and looping it around the wire to create a smooth, closely woven surface. Use this technique to weave the Fused Flowers, the Candle Sconce, the Woven Chair and the Woven Bottle.

Method C

Follow Method B but reverse the weave, this time passing the wire under each strut before looping it around the wire to create ridges in the weave. This technique will give the same result as method B except that the rib will be on the outside, not the inside.

CHICKEN WIRE TECHNIQUES

Chicken wire is a fantastic medium as it is cheap, attractive and readily available. Its malleability and lightness make it suitable for creating large structures, and as such it is commonly used by sculptors. For ease of explanation, the instructions refer to struts (the horizontal, twisted wires in the hexagons) and strands (the single wires). When working with chicken wire, it is advisable to wear gloves. Finish off any project made of chicken wire by tucking away all the sharp ends.

BINDING CHICKEN WIRE
Method A

Place a length of wire along the edge of the chicken wire. Loop a thinner binding wire around the length of wire and the chicken wire to bind them together. Use this technique to bind the chicken wire in the Picture Frame, to bind the sides and bottom of the Utility Rack, and to bind the rim of the Lantern and its lid.

Method B

When binding diagonally, it is convenient to bind along the diagonal strands of the chicken wire. If a more acute diagonal is needed, as for the top of the Utility Rack, allow 2 cm (¾ in) excess chicken wire. Bind evenly around the length of wire, taking in each strand or strut of chicken wire as you come to it. Trim and wrap any ends around the length of wire using round-nosed pliers.

TRANSFORMING THE HOLE SHAPES

The hexagonal shape of the holes gives chicken wire plenty of moulding potential, which can be increased still further by breaking the rigidity of the horizontal struts.

Heart Shapes

Hold the centre of each strut in turn with round-nosed jewellery pliers and twist up the wire to each side to create a cleft in the centre. When this process is repeated a pattern of heart shapes will emerge.

Brick Wall

Insert general-purpose pliers into the holes in the chicken wire so that the sides of the pliers are up against the struts. Pull the handles gently apart to transform each hexagon into a rectangle. You will need to work carefully to stop the mesh buckling.

Fishing Net

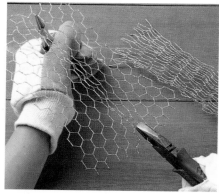

Hold the chicken wire securely with small pliers and pull it with general-purpose pliers to elongate the holes and create a fishing net effect. You could hook the chicken wire over nails hammered into a piece of wood if you were stretching a larger area.

JOINING CHICKEN WIRE

1 Cut the chicken wire at the point just before the wire strands twist into struts so that one edge is a row of projecting double strands and the other edge is a row of projecting twisted struts.

2 Place the piece of chicken wire with the projecting struts on top of the other piece so that they overlap slightly and the rows of struts lie on top of each other. Using round-nosed pliers, wrap each projecting strand around the corresponding strand on the uppermost piece of chicken wire.

3 Twist the overlapping struts together using round-nosed pliers.

SHAPING CHICKEN WIRE

Depending on the type of shape and the rigidity of structure required, chicken wire can be shaped with the struts running either horizontally or vertically. Generally, for a stronger, fatter shape, work with the struts running horizontally and, for a longer, more elegant shape, work with the struts running vertically. Although any number of shapes can be made, the ones described here can be used for making the Lantern project.

Shaping with the Struts Running Vertically

1 Using general-purpose pliers, squeeze the struts together to form the neck, pulling all the time to elongate the wires.

2 To make the bulge, stretch the holes by inserting general-purpose pliers as described for the brick wall, but only stretch a little for a more elegant shape.

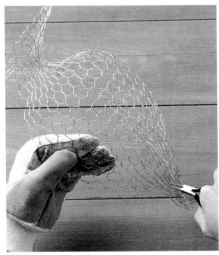

3 Using round-nosed pliers, squeeze the struts together to make the bottom tip, pulling to elongate the wires.

Shaping with the Struts Running Horizontally

1 Transform all the hexagons to heart shapes. To contract the wire that will become the neck, squash together the cleft in each heart shape with round-nosed pliers and mould with your thumbs.

2 To make the bulge in the body of the structure, mould with your fingers from inside, pressing outwards. Using round-nosed pliers grip and pull the wires outwards.

3 To make the bottom tip, squash together the clefts as for the neck, contracting them more tightly to form a tight core.

LOO ROLL HOLDER

TRANSFORM ONE SIMPLE, FUNCTIONAL OBJECT INTO ANOTHER WITH THIS CHARMING TOILET ROLL HOLDER MADE FROM A WIRE COAT-HANGER. THE LESS EXPERIENCED WIREWORKER IS ADVISED TO START WITH THIS PROJECT. HEARTS ARE A TRADITIONAL MOTIF IN FOLK ART DESIGNS AND TRANSFORM FUNCTIONAL OBJECTS INTO WARM, PERSONAL ONES. ADAPT THE BASIC DESIGN TO MAKE OTHER BATHROOM ACCESSORIES, SUCH AS TOOTHBRUSH, GLASS OR SOAP DISH HOLDERS. IF YOU PREFER, YOU COULD USE GALVANIZED OR PLASTIC-COATED GARDEN WIRE INSTEAD OF A WIRE COAT-HANGER.

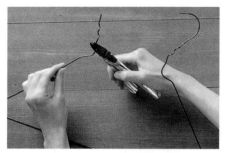

1 Unwind the coat-hanger and cut off the hook and twisted wire. Straighten the remaining wire using parallel pliers.

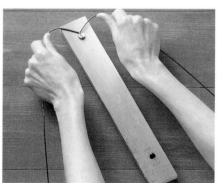

2 Drill a hole in a piece of wood and wind in a screw. Wrap the wire around the screw halfway along its length. Tighten the screw so that it holds the wire securely in place as you mould the curves of the heart shape.

3 Allow 6 cm (2½ in) between the eye and the bottom of the heart. Twist the wire together twice at the bottom of the heart. Bend out the remaining wires at right angles.

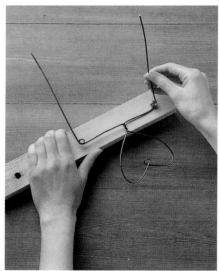

4 Unscrew the heart and replace the screw in the wood. Measure 6 cm (2½ in) from the bottom of the heart along each wire. Wrap each wire once around the screw at this point and bend up the end at a right angle.

5 Using permanent marker pen, mark each remaining length of wire at intervals of 8 cm (3 in), 3 cm (1¼ in), 3 cm (1¼ in), 2 cm (¾ in) and 2 cm (¾ in). The measurements may have to vary slightly depending on how much wire is left. Bend the wire into right angles at the marked points, so the ends that will hold the toilet roll point inwards. To decorate, loosely wrap a length of 0.8 mm (0.031 in) galvanized wire around the whole structure.

MATERIALS AND EQUIPMENT YOU WILL NEED

WIRE COAT-HANGER • WIRE CUTTERS • PARALLEL PLIERS • PIECE OF WOOD • DRILL • SCREW • RULER • PERMANENT MARKER PEN • GENERAL-PURPOSE PLIERS • GALVANIZED WIRE 0.8 MM (0.031 IN) THICK

POCKET CLIPS

ADORN YOUR POCKETS WITH THESE HIGHLY ORIGINAL AND DECORATIVE CLIPS THAT WILL ADD A TOUCH OF FLAIR TO THE MOST ORDINARY OF JACKETS. DESIGN YOUR OWN CLIPS FOR THE TOP POCKET OR LAPEL OF A MAN'S JACKET OR A TEENAGER'S SCHOOL BLAZER. YOU COULD COPY AN EXISTING EMBLEM OR LOGO OR EVEN SCULPT A NAME OR WORD. A SMALLER DESIGN MADE IN FINE WIRE WOULD MAKE AN ATTRACTIVE TIE CLIP. GALVANIZED WIRE HAS BEEN USED HERE WHICH COULD BE SPRAYED WITH METALLIC CAR PAINT. FOR A MORE SOPHISTICATED LOOK USE GOLD- OR SILVER-PLATED WIRE.

1 Cut 1 m (40 in) of 1.2 mm (0.047 in) galvanized wire. Using round-nosed pliers, make a coil at one end. Bend the wire out to make an S-shape, referring to diagram 1. Square off the loop below the coil with half-round pliers.

2 Bend the wire in to form one side of a neck, then make a large loop in the wire. Make a mirror image loop and coil on the other side of the large loop and cut off any excess wire.

3 Fold the structure in half at the neck and bend the top of the large loop at both sides to make shoulders. Nip in the bottom of the large loop to make a scallop shape. The large loop should measure approximately 11 cm (4½ in) from top to bottom.

DIAGRAM 1

4 Using the 0.65 mm (0.025 in) wire, bind the coils together. Bind the neck together for 1 cm (½ in).

MATERIALS AND EQUIPMENT YOU WILL NEED

GALVANIZED WIRE 1.2 MM (0.047 IN) AND 0.65 MM (0.025 IN) THICK • RULER • WIRE CUTTERS • ROUND-NOSED PLIERS • HALF-ROUND PLIERS

PICTURE FRAME

THIS LIGHT AND AIRY PICTURE FRAME IS MADE FROM THICK ALUMINIUM WIRE, WHICH IS SOFT AND BENDS EASILY TO FORM THE FILIGREE FRAME SURROUND. THE PASTEL RIBBON AND OLD-FASHIONED PICTURE CREATE A VICTORIAN EFFECT. IT IS VERY EASY TO CHANGE THE RIBBON AND PICTURE TO FIT IN WITH ANY SETTING AS THE FRAME CONTAINS NO GLASS. SUBTLY COLOURED PICTURES AND BLACK AND WHITE PHOTOGRAPHS ARE ESPECIALLY EFFECTIVE. CHOOSE A RIBBON THAT IS THIN ENOUGH TO THREAD EASILY THROUGH THE WIRE MESH AND THAT MATCHES OR CONTRASTS WITH THE PICTURE.

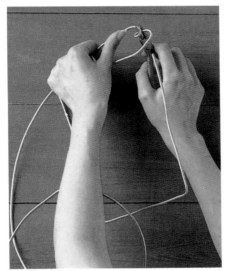

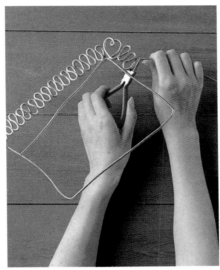

1 Using round-nosed pliers, bend the 3.25 mm (0.128 in) aluminium wire into a rectangle 15 x 20 cm (6 x 8 in). At the fourth corner, form a heart shape. Do not cut off the wire.

2 Bend the wire into a series of filigree loops to fit along each side of the frame. Form a heart at each corner.

3 Leave 1 cm (½ in) of wire spare at the last corner and cut off. ▶

MATERIALS AND EQUIPMENT YOU WILL NEED
ROUND-NOSED PLIERS • SOFT ALUMINIUM WIRE 3.25 MM (0.128 IN) AND 1 MM (0.039 IN) THICK • RULER • WIRE CUTTERS • SMALL-GAUGE CHICKEN WIRE • GLOVES (OPTIONAL) • GALVANIZED WIRE 1.65 MM (0.065 IN) THICK • PERMANENT MARKER PEN • RIBBON

4 Cut a piece of chicken wire 15 x 40 cm (6 x 16 in) and fold it in half. Bend the filigree out of the way and use 1 mm (0.039 in) aluminium wire to bind the chicken wire to the inner rectangle (see Basic Techniques).

5 Bend the filigree back into place and bind onto the inner rectangle.

6 To make the support, cut a 48 cm (19 in) length of galvanized wire. Using permanent marker pen, mark the wire at intervals of 18 cm (7 in), 6 cm (2½ in), 6 cm (2½ in) and 18 cm (7 in). Bend the wire into a crossed triangle shape, making a loop in the centre and a loop at each end. Cut two short pieces of wire and make a loop at each end. Link the two pieces together and close the loop firmly.

7 Thread a piece of ribbon around the edges of the chicken wire, looping it around the frame at each corner so that it lies flat.

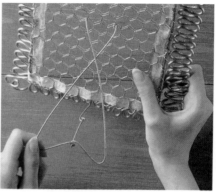

8 Attach the support to the frame by opening the loops slightly and then closing them around the chicken wire about two-thirds of the way up from the bottom. Attach one end of the two short linked pieces to the loop in the bottom of the support and the other end to the base of the frame. This piece prevents the support from collapsing and allows the frame to be folded flat.

9 Position your picture on the frame and secure it by threading a ribbon through the wire from the back, and looping it around the corners, as shown.

UTILITY RACK

THE SHELF AT THE BOTTOM OF THIS USEFUL AND SIMPLY DESIGNED RACK IS WIDE ENOUGH TO HOLD FOUR FOOD CANS. STRIPPED OF THEIR LABELS, THE CANS MAKE ATTRACTIVE STORAGE CONTAINERS THAT COMPLEMENT THE DESIGN OF THE RACK. ALTERNATIVELY, THE SHELF WILL HOLD THREE SMALL PLANT POTS.

HANG THE RACK IN THE HOUSE, STUDIO, GARAGE OR SHED. SCREWED TO THE WALL AT EACH LOOPED POINT, IT WILL BE QUITE SECURE AND CAPABLE OF HOLDING A CONSIDERABLE WEIGHT. THE LITTLE BASKET HANGING FROM THE BOTTOM IS MADE FROM A SMALL CHINESE SIEVE.

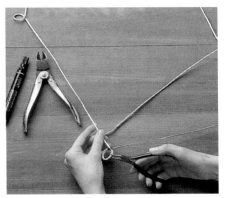

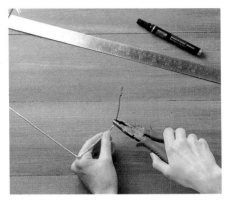

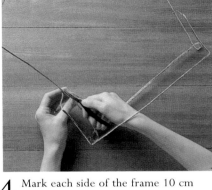

1 To make the frame, cut a 2 m (79 in) length of straining wire. Twist the ends tightly to stop them unravelling and, with permanent marker pen, mark the wire at intervals of 29.5 cm (11½ in), 5 cm (2 in), 33 cm (13 in), 5 cm (2 in), 25 cm (10 in), 5 cm (2 in), 25 cm (10 in), 5 cm (2 in), 33 cm (13 in), 5 cm (2 in) and 29.5 cm (11½ in). Using round-nosed pliers, make a loop with each 5 cm (2 in) section, making sure that the pen marks match up and that all the loops face outwards (see diagram 1).

2 Using the 0.65 mm (0.025 in) galvanized wire, bind the two 29.5 cm (11½ in) sections together to make the bottom of the frame.

3 To make the shelf, cut a 72 cm (29 in) length of straining wire and mark it at intervals of 2 cm (1 in), 9 cm (3½ in), 10 cm (4 in), 30 cm (12 in), 10 cm (4 in), 9 cm (3½ in) and 2 cm (1 in). Using general-purpose pliers, bend the wire at right angles at these points (see diagram 2).

DIAGRAM 1

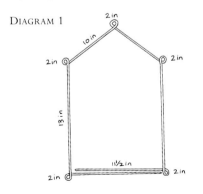

4 Mark each side of the frame 10 cm (4 in) from the bottom. Twist the 2 cm (1 in) ends of the shelf wire tightly around the frame at these points.

▶

DIAGRAM 2

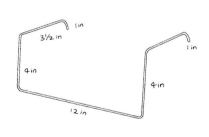

MATERIALS AND EQUIPMENT YOU WILL NEED

STRAINING WIRE • RULER • WIRE CUTTERS • PERMANENT MARKER PEN • ROUND-NOSED PLIERS • GALVANIZED WIRE 1.65 MM (0.065 IN) AND 0.65 MM (0.025 IN) THICK • GENERAL-PURPOSE PLIERS • TACKING WIRE • SMALL-GAUGE CHICKEN WIRE • GLOVES

DIAGRAM 4

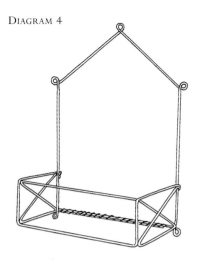

5 To make the rim and sides of the shelf, cut a 104 cm (41 in) length of 1.65 mm (0.065 in) galvanized wire and mark it at intervals of 2 cm (1 in), 13 cm (5 in), 9 cm (3½ in), 13 cm (5 in), 30 cm (12 in), 13 cm (5 in), 9 cm (3½ in), 13 cm (5 in) and 2 cm (1 in). Using round-nosed pliers, make a loop with the 2 cm (1 in) section at each end of the wire. Bend the wire at the 13 cm (5 in) and 9 cm (3½ in) points at each end at 45° angles to form the side crosses of the shelf. Bend the 30 cm (12 in) section in the middle at right angles to form the top rim (see diagram 3).

DIAGRAM 3

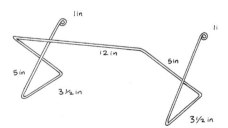

6 Tack the loops at the ends of the rim wire to the 10 cm (4 in) markings on the sides of the main frame. Tack each corner of the side crosses to the frame (see diagram 4).

7 Wearing gloves for protection, lay the frame onto the flat piece of chicken wire and cut around the frame. Allow 30 cm (12 in) at the bottom for wrapping around the shelf, so that there is a double thickness of chicken wire at the front of the shelf where it tucks inside. Using 0.65 mm (0.025 in) galvanized wire, bind the edges of the chicken wire to the frame (see Basic Techniques). Wrap any rough edges at the top around the frame before binding. Bind the shelf firmly to the frame as you bind on the chicken wire and remove the tacking wire.

HIPPY HAPPY NECKLACE

WIRE COMES IN MANY FORMS AND APPEARS HERE IN DISGUISE AS PIPE CLEANERS. THE RANGE OF PIPE CLEANERS USED IN THIS PROJECT IS AVAILABLE AT EDUCATIONAL TOY SHOPS. THE NECKLACES ARE GREAT FUN TO CREATE AND ARE THE PERFECT PROJECT TO MAKE WITH CHILDREN. MAKE MATCHING ACCESSORIES USING CLIP-ON EARRING BACKS AND HAIRSLIDE BASES. GLUE A SMALL PIPE CLEANER FLOWER ONTO EACH EARRING BACK AND LARGER ONES ONTO THE SLIDE BASES. TO MAKE A BRACELET, ATTACH FLOWERS TO A LARGE FURRY PIPE CLEANER IN THE SAME WAY AS FOR THE NECKLACE.

1 Using round-nosed pliers, make small flowers from plain pipe cleaners. Make the centres of the flowers by straightening stripy paper clips and coiling them into spirals (see Basic Techniques). Then bend a furry pipe cleaner with your fingers to make a five-petalled flower. Twist the ends together. Coil a plain pipe cleaner and stripy paper clip into spirals to make the centre of the large flower.

2 To attach the centres, cut a length of twisty wire tape and tie a knot in it. Thread it through the flower so the knot is at the front and there is a long end behind.

4 Form a loop at each end of the pipe cleaner and attach twisty wire tape to each loop. Form two paper clips into cones. Trim them, then slide them onto the ends.

3 Bend a thick, bumpy pipe cleaner into a semicircle. Bind the small flowers to the pipe cleaner with the twisty tape, tucking in the ends behind the flowers. Bind the large flower to a paper clip and clip onto the pipe cleaner.

5 Bend the ends of straightened clips into coils. Join the double spirals together to make two chains. Make a hook and eye catch from paper clips. Attach the chains to the ends of the pipe cleaner, then attach the hook and eye catch.

MATERIALS AND EQUIPMENT YOU WILL NEED
ROUND-NOSED PLIERS • PLAIN, FURRY, AND THICK, BUMPY PIPE CLEANERS • STRIPY AND COLOURED PAPER CLIPS •
TWISTY WIRE TAPE • WIRE CUTTERS

GREETINGS CARDS

A HOMEMADE CARD MAKES A PERSONAL GIFT THAT WILL BE CHERISHED. OFFER THIS CHERUB CARD TO THAT SPECIAL SOMEONE ON VALENTINE'S DAY. APPLY YOUR CREATIVITY TO MAKE WIRE CARDS FOR BIRTHDAYS, CHRISTMAS, EASTER AND MOTHER'S DAY USING APPROPRIATE MOTIFS. METALLIC SPRAY PAINTS CAN BE BOUGHT FROM CAR ACCESSORY SHOPS AND ADD A COLOURFUL LUSTRE TO THE WIRE, AS CAN BE SEEN IN THE SEASHORE MOBILE PROJECT. IF YOU ARE DELIVERING YOUR CARD BY HAND, WHY NOT WRITE THE RECIPIENT'S NAME IN WIRE AND ATTACH IT TO THE ENVELOPE?

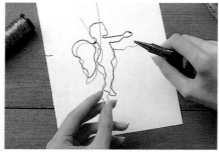

1 Cut a 22 x 32 cm (8½ x 13 in) rectangle of red card and a 14.5 x 21 cm (5¾ x 8¼ in) rectangle of pink card. Score a line down the centre of the red card and fold. Draw around the small heart template on page 93 in the centre of the red card, 2.5 cm (1 in) from the bottom. Draw around the large heart template in the centre of the pink card, 1.5 cm (⅝ in) from the bottom. Cut out the hearts and reserve the cut-out hearts. Erase all the pencil marks. Spray the bottom edge of the pink card gold.

2 To make the cherubs, use round-nosed pliers to bend the 0.65 mm (0.025 in) galvanized wire around the template on page 93. Bind the cherub shapes where the wings join the body. Then make two hearts from 1.2 mm (0.047 in) wire.

3 Use a pin to make pairs of holes around the cherubs and one of the hearts, where they will be positioned on the pink card.

4 Thread the nylon through the holes in the card from behind to attach the cherubs and heart. Secure at the back with masking tape. Hang the second heart from the first with cotton thread so that it hangs in the heart-shaped hole. Glue the pink card onto the red card. Glue the pink heart onto the inside of the card so that, when the card is closed, the inner heart is pink.

MATERIALS AND EQUIPMENT YOU WILL NEED

RED AND PINK CARD • RULER • PENCIL • SCISSORS • SCALPEL • ERASER • GOLD SPRAY PAINT • ROUND-NOSED PLIERS • GALVANIZED WIRE 1.2 MM (0.047 IN) AND 0.65 MM (0.025 IN) THICK • WIRE CUTTERS • DRESSMAKING PINS • THIN NYLON THREAD • MASKING TAPE • RED COTTON THREAD • PAPER GLUE

FUSED FLOWERS

FASHION YOURSELF A BUNCH OF FABULOUS FLOWERS, WOVEN OUT OF RICHLY COLOURED FUSE WIRE. ONCE YOU HAVE MASTERED THE FLOWER DESCRIBED IN THE STEP INSTRUCTIONS, ADAPT THE DESIGN TO MAKE THE TWO VARIATIONS SHOWN IN THE PICTURE. ENAMELLED COPPER WIRE COMES IN A VAST ARRAY OF COLOURS, SO YOU CAN ADD LEAVES AND TENDRILS BY SPIRALLING AND COILING THE ENDS OF LENGTHS OF THICKER AND DARKER ENAMELLED COPPER WIRE. DISPLAY THE FLOWERS TO DRAMATIC EFFECT IN A METALLIC VASE OR IN THE WOVEN BOTTLE, WHICH IS MADE USING THE SAME WEAVING TECHNIQUES.

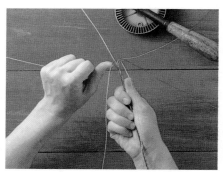

1 Cut six 50 cm (20 in) lengths of 1 mm (0.039 in) wire. Twist together along half the length using a hand drill (see Basic Techniques) to form the stem. Bend back the wires loosely.

3 Weave a bulb-shaped stamen, 2.5 cm (1 in) high and 1.5 cm (⅝ in) wide.

5 Using a different-coloured wire, weave a flower shape 6 cm (2½ in) high.

2 Holding the wires in one hand, attach a length of 0.65 mm (0.025 in) wire to the centre. Start weaving around the six wires (see Basic Techniques).

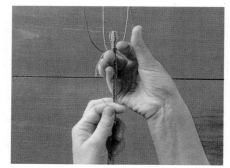

4 Bend each wire back up around the stamen between your finger and thumb.

6 Using round-nosed pliers, bend each remaining length of wire to form a loose coil. Finally, bind the stem with several lengths of fine enamelled copper wire.

MATERIALS AND EQUIPMENT YOU WILL NEED

ENAMELLED COPPER WIRE 1 MM (0.039 IN) THICK AND 0.65 MM (0.025 IN) THICK IN TWO COLOURS • RULER • WIRE CUTTERS • HAND DRILL • ROUND-NOSED PLIERS

SPOON RACK

THE ELEGANCE OF THIS FRESH GREEN RACK WILL ADD STYLE TO YOUR HOME AND ENSURE THAT YOUR KITCHEN IMPLEMENTS SUCH AS BRUSHES AND SPOONS ARE ALWAYS CLOSE AT HAND. THE SIMPLICITY OF THE DESIGN IS REFLECTED IN THE CHOICE OF MATERIALS. GARDEN WIRE IS INEXPENSIVE AND READILY AVAILABLE, AND IT COMES IN MANY DIFFERENT THICKNESSES AND COLOURS.

ALTERNATIVELY, YOU COULD USE GALVANIZED OR TINNED COPPER WIRE. THE CLOVER LEAF, WHICH IS USED FOR THE HOLDERS, IS A RECURRENT MOTIF IN WIREWORK PROJECTS AND CAN BE FORMED AROUND CYLINDRICAL OBJECTS OF DIFFERENT SIZES SUCH AS A WOODEN SPOON, BROOM HANDLE OR A ROLLING PIN (SEE BOTTLE CARRIER AND HOOK RACK).

1 Cut three 1 m (40 in) lengths of thick garden wire. Wrap one end of each wire three times around a rolling pin. Using round-nosed pliers, make a small loop in the coiled end of each wire large enough to take a screw. Shape the coils to make a spiral in each wire. Bend back the wire from one of the lengths at a right angle to make the central stem.

2 To make the spoon holders, cut three 58 cm (23 in) lengths of wire. Bend each wire at a right angle 12 cm (5 in) from one end.

3 In the next section of wire, make a row of three circles by wrapping the wire one and a half times around a piece of copper piping (or similar tube) for each circle.

4 Bend the remaining wire away from the third circle at a right angle. Bend the three circles round to form a clover shape and bind the long end of wire around the 12 cm (5 in) end for 7 cm (2¾ in). Do not cut off the ends.

5 Arrange the three spiralled wires together with the right-angled one in the centre. Measure 30 cm (12 in) from the right angle on the central stem and mark this point. Cut a 36 cm (14 in) length of wire and make a small loop in one end. Leave 2 cm (¾ in) next to the loop, then bind the wire tightly around the spiralled wires, upwards from the marked point (see diagram 1).

DIAGRAM 1

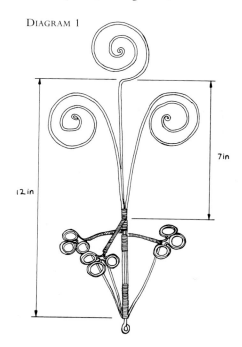

12 in

7 in

MATERIALS AND EQUIPMENT YOU WILL NEED

THICK GARDEN WIRE • RULER • WIRE CUTTERS • ROLLING PIN • ROUND-NOSED PLIERS • PIECE OF COPPER PIPING • PERMANENT MARKER PEN

6 Measure 18 cm (7 in) from the right
angle of the central stem and, using
the excess wire on one of the clover
shapes, bind it onto the stem at this point.
Bind upwards for 2 cm (¾ in) and cut off
the wire. Bind on the second clover shape
2 cm (¾ in) below the first in the same
way. Attach the third clover shape below
the second, binding downwards for 4 cm
(1½ in). Make a bend halfway along the
stems of the second and third clover
shapes to angle them inwards slightly.

7 Bend up the three stem wires at the
bottom and bind each to the neck of
one of the clover shapes. Cut off the ends.
Screw the spoon holder to the wall
through the loop in each spiral and at the
bottom of the stem.

WIRE BASKET

THIS STURDY BASKET IS PARTICULARLY SUITABLE FOR GATHERING VEGETABLES FROM THE GARDEN. THE WIRE MESH ALLOWS THE SOIL TO FALL THROUGH AND, BECAUSE THE WIRE IS GALVANIZED AND RUSTPROOF, THE DIRTY VEGETABLES WITHIN IT CAN BE HOSED DOWN IN THE GARDEN. IN THE PAST, WIRE BASKETS WERE USED FOR COLLECTING CLAMS FROM THE SEASHORE OR CARRYING BREAD HOME FROM THE SHOPS. FEW DESIGNS ARE PRODUCED TODAY, WITH THE EXCEPTION OF KITCHENWARE BASKETS FOR SALADS AND FRYING, MANY OF WHICH ARE COLLAPSIBLE. WEAR GLOVES WHEN WORKING WITH CHICKEN WIRE TO PROTECT YOUR HANDS.

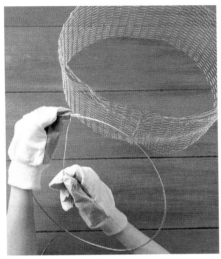

1 To make the cylinder, cut a piece of chicken wire 28 x 88 cm (11 x 35 in). Form it into an oval and join the short edges together (see Basic Techniques). Cut a 95 cm (37 in) length of straining wire and form it into an oval that will fit snugly inside the chicken wire cylinder. Bind the ends together with 0.65 mm (0.025 in) galvanized wire.

2 To shape the basket, count up ten holes from the bottom of the cylinder. This section will be the base. Bend all the holes into heart shapes (see Basic Techniques).

3 To make the base support, cut a 70 cm (27½ in) length of straining wire and bind into an oval.

4 Cut two 18 cm (7 in) lengths of 1.65 mm (0.065 in) wire and two 23 cm (9 in) lengths. Using round-nosed pliers, attach the wires to the oval to form a grid, binding where the wires cross.

5 Push the bottom edges of the basket together and bind with 0.65 mm (0.025 in) galvanized wire to close up the base neatly.

▶

MATERIALS AND EQUIPMENT YOU WILL NEED

SMALL-GAUGE CHICKEN WIRE • WIRE CUTTERS • GLOVES • RULER • STRAINING WIRE • GALVANIZED WIRE 1.65 MM (0.065 IN) AND 0.65 MM (0.025 IN) THICK • ROUND-NOSED PLIERS • PERMANENT MARKER PEN • TACKING WIRE • BROOMSTICK

6 Position the base support on the bottom of the basket and bind it onto the chicken wire all the way round.

7 Place the large oval of straining wire inside the basket 5 cm (2 in) from the top. Fold the chicken wire over it to reinforce the top rim of the basket.

8 Mark a 55 cm (21½ in) length of straining wire but do not cut it. Tack the end to one side of the basket and bend to form the handle. Secure the wire where you have marked it to the other side of the basket. Wrap the next section of straining wire ten times around a broomstick to form ten loops (see Basic Techniques). Bind these loops around the basket to where the handle wire is tacked.

9 Bend the wire over the basket to double the handle. Bend the next section of wire to form a three-petalled decoration, as shown, and bind it to the basket. Loop the handle across again and make another three-petalled decoration on the other side.

10 Bend the wire back over the basket to form a fourth handle loop. Using the broomstick, make ten more loops in the wire and bind around the basket.

11 Using 0.65 mm (0.025 in) galvanized wire, bind the four handle wires together at the top, tucking the ends inside.

CHANDELIER

CREATE THIS SPLENDID CHANDELIER TO HANG OVER YOUR DINING TABLE. THE ELEGANT STAR-SHAPED FRAME HOLDS LIGHTS MADE BY PLACING A THIN LAYER OF OLIVE OIL AND A FLOATING WICK INSIDE GLASSES HALF-FILLED WITH WATER. TINT THE WATER WITH FOOD DYE. CHOOSE GLASSES WITH TAPERING SIDES, SO THEY DON'T SLIP THROUGH THE HOLDERS, OR USE BABY FOOD JARS WITH NECKS WIDE ENOUGH TO TAKE THE THICKNESS OF THE WIRE. THE LONG LENGTH OF ALUMINIUM WIRE NEEDED FOR THIS PROJECT IS QUITE DIFFICULT TO WORK WITH IN THE EARLY STAGES. WEAR GLOVES TO PREVENT THE WIRE FROM COLOURING YOUR HANDS.

1 Using permanent marker pen, mark the 3.25 mm (0.128 in) aluminium wire at intervals of 55 cm (21½ in), 5 cm (2 in), 55 cm (21½ in), 5 cm (2 in), 55 cm (21½ in), 5 cm (2 in), 55 cm (21½ in), 5 cm (2 in), 55 cm (21½ in), 5 cm (2 in) and 5 cm (2 in).

2 Using round-nosed pliers, bend each 5 cm (2 in) section into a loop, leaving the last 5 cm (2 in) straight for joining. Weave the long sections over and under each other to form a star shape. Bind the last 5 cm (2 in) to the beginning of the wire, using 1 mm (0.039 in) aluminium wire. Bind each loop closed.

3 To even up the star shape, divide each 55 cm (21½ in) length of wire into three equal sections of just over 18 cm (7 in), and mark the points. Match up the marks where the wires cross and bind together at these points using 1 mm (0.039 in) wire.

4 Enlarge the templates on page 93 to size by photocopying them at 150%. It is essential that all the pieces are enlarged by the same percentage.

5 Cut 30 33 cm (13 in) lengths of 3.25 mm (0.128 in) wire. Using round-nosed pliers, carefully bend 15 of these lengths around the nosed double coil template.

▶

MATERIALS AND EQUIPMENT YOU WILL NEED

GLOVES • SOFT ALUMINIUM WIRE 3.25 MM (0.128 IN) AND 1 MM (0.039 IN) THICK • RULER • PERMANENT MARKER PEN • ROUND-NOSED PLIERS • WIRE CUTTERS • PHOTOCOPIER AND PAPER • FIVE GLASSES OR JARS AT LEAST 5.5 CM (2¼ IN) IN DIAMETER • ONE GLASS OR JAR AT LEAST 6 CM (2½ IN) IN DIAMETER • SIX BATH PLUG CHAINS • METAL RING

6 Using round-nosed pliers, bend the remaining 15 lengths of wire around the templates on page 93 to make five double coils, five arched double coils and five single looped coils.

7 To make the glass holders, cut five 50 cm (20 in) lengths of 3.25 mm (0.128 in) wire. Wrap each around one of the 5.5 cm (2¼ in) glasses or jars. Wrap the wire around twice and overlap the ends. Use the template on page 93 to coil the wire at each end. To make the central glass holder, cut a 60 cm (24 in) length of wire and wrap it three times around the larger glass or jar to make a plain coil.

8 Using five short lengths of 1 mm (0.039 in) aluminium wire, bind the five double coils onto the central holder.

9 Bind the double coils together where the sides touch to make the raised central piece. Then bind alternate arched double coils and single looped coils around the edge.

DIAGRAM 1

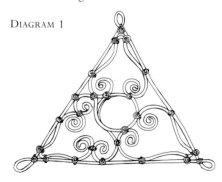

10 Bind three nosed double coils to each small glass holder: bind one nosed double coil to the coils on the glass holder and the other two to the ring. Position each structure inside the points of the star frame so that the noses of the nosed double coils fit into the corners and the coils of the glass holder face towards the tip. Bind in place (see diagram 1).

11 Bind the central piece to the star frame at all the points of contact. Attach a bath plug chain to each of the five points where the wires of the star frame cross. Attach the hooks at the ends of the chains to a metal ring and close up. Attach the sixth bath plug chain to the top of the ring for hanging. Place the glasses or jars in the holders.

GARDEN TRAY

ONE OF THE GREAT THINGS ABOUT WIRE IS THAT IT PROVIDES STRUCTURE TO OTHERWISE FLIMSY MATERIALS. HERE THE WIRE IS COMPLETELY COVERED WITH RAFFIA TO CREATE A ROMANTICALLY RUSTIC TRAY. A READY-MADE MAT FORMS THE BASE, BUT YOU COULD MAKE YOUR OWN USING 48 CM (19 IN) STICKS OF EQUAL THICKNESS. BIND THEM TOGETHER WITH RAFFIA TO MAKE A MAT APPROXIMATELY 38 CM (16 IN) WIDE. YOU COULD USE ANOTHER TYPE OF MAT AS LONG AS IT IS RIGID ALONG ITS LENGTH. USE THE TRAY FOR GARDENING OR AS AN ATTRACTIVE HOLDER FOR SEVERAL POT PLANTS.

1 Cut two 1 m (40 in) lengths of straining wire. Using permanent marker pen, mark each wire at intervals of 26 cm (10 in), 5 cm (2 in), 38 cm (16 in), 5 cm (2 in) and 26 cm (10 in). Using parallel pliers, bend each wire at the marked points to create the shape of two carrying handles. The two 26 cm (10 in) sections double up to form the base. The two 5 cm (2 in) sections make the sides and the 38 cm (16 in) section curves over the top. Hold each handle together at the base with double-sided sticky tape.

2 To make the hearts, cut two 1 m (40 in) lengths of wire and mark at intervals of 37 cm (15 in), 26 cm (10 in) and 37 cm (15 in). Make each 26 cm (10 in) section into a heart shape and cross the wires over at the marked points. Bend up the wire and secure with tape. Wrap the heart wires and the handles with tape, then bind them with raffia.

3 Using round-nosed pliers, bend the ends of the heart wires into coils, so that they will fit inside the handles.

4 Position the end of the mat inside one of the handles and bind in place with raffia. Thread the raffia between the sticks of the mat and around the sides and base of the handle. Position the heart wire inside the handle and bind in place where the coils touch the sides and the heart touches the bottom. Bind the second handle and heart wire to the other end of the mat.

5 Make two bundles of twigs and bind tightly to the top of the handles with double-sided sticky tape. Wrap with raffia to cover all the tape.

MATERIALS AND EQUIPMENT YOU WILL NEED
STRAINING WIRE • RULER • WIRE CUTTERS • PERMANENT MARKER PEN • PARALLEL PLIERS • ROUND-NOSED PLIERS •
DOUBLE-SIDED STICKY TAPE • SCISSORS • RAFFIA • STICK MAT • TWIGS

SEASHORE MOBILE

A MARINE THEME IS IDEAL FOR A MOBILE AS THE GENTLE MOVEMENT SUFFUSES THE SEA CREATURES WITH AN "UNDERWATER" GRACE. HERE SEAHORSES, STARFISH, DOLPHINS AND FISHES UNDULATE AROUND THE CENTRAL FIGURE OF A CRAB. WIRE IS AN EXCELLENT MATERIAL FOR MOBILE-MAKING AS IT IS LIGHT AND CAN BE FASHIONED INTO ANY IMAGINABLE SHAPE. SPRAY PAINT THE WIRES DIFFERENT COLOURS TO GIVE THEM A SUBTLE, VARIEGATED HUE. DESIGN YOUR OWN MOBILES ON DIFFERENT THEMES. FORM STARS, SUN, MOON AND CLOUDS FOR A CELESTIAL MOBILE OR PINK AND RED HEARTS AND CHERUBS FOR A ROMANTIC THEME.

1 To make the small supports, cut two 46 cm (18 in) lengths of 2 mm (0.078 in) wire. Bend each wire into an arch and form a coil at each end using round-nosed pliers. Bend a curve in the wire near each coil using half-round pliers.

2 To make the main supports, cut two 74 cm (29 in) lengths of 2 mm (0.078 in) wire. Bend each wire into an arch, form a coil at each end and bend waves in the wire beside each coil.

3 Cut a 3 cm (1¼ in) length of 2 mm (0.078 in) wire. Using the half-round pliers, bend the wire round to make a ring. Cross the main support wires so that they meet exactly in the centre and tape together, with the ring at the top. Wrap with 0.65 mm (0.025 in) wire to secure the join, completely covering the tape.

4 Enlarge the templates on page 94 to size by photocopying them at 180%. It is essential that all the pieces are enlarged by the same percentage.

5 To make the starfish and shell, cut three pieces of 1.65 mm (0.065 in) wire: 22 cm (8½ in), 32 cm (13 in) and 50 cm (20 in) long. Using the templates, form the 22 cm (8½ in) length of wire into a shell, the 32 cm (13 in) length into a small starfish and the 50 cm (20 in) length into a large starfish. Bind the ends together using the thinnest wire.

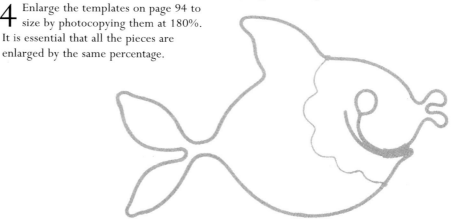

MATERIALS AND EQUIPMENT YOU WILL NEED
GALVANIZED WIRE 2 MM (0.078 IN), 1.65 MM (0.065 IN), 1.2 MM (0.047 IN) AND 0.65 MM (0.025 IN) THICK • RULER • WIRE CUTTERS • ROUND-NOSED PLIERS • HALF-ROUND PLIERS • DOUBLE-SIDED STICKY TAPE • PHOTOCOPIER AND PAPER • CAR SPRAY PAINTS • NYLON THREAD • SCISSORS

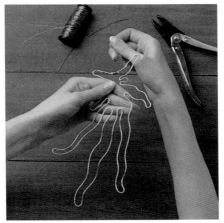

6 Cut a 90 cm (36 in) length of
1.65 mm (0.065 in) wire and form
into a seaweed shape. Bind the ends
together using the thinnest wire.

7 Use both the round-nosed and half-
round pliers to bend a 90 cm (36 in)
length of 1.65 mm (0.065 in) wire into a
seahorse shape.

8 Bind the ends of the wire together at
the top of the seahorse's head using
the thinnest wire. Use the same wire to
make the seahorse's dorsal fin. Loop the
wire around the wire of the seahorse's
back to make a series of arches. Nip a
point in each arch.

9 To make the fish, cut two pieces of
1.65 mm (0.065 in) wire, 71 cm
(28 in) and 1 m (40 in) long. When you
have completed the outline of the large
fish, add a wavy line of the thinnest wire
between the head and body. Bind the point
where the head meets the body, then wrap
along the bottom of the body. Extend the
wire across the body, bind the join at the
top and cut off. Complete the small fish
with a wavy line of the thinnest wire
between the head and the body.

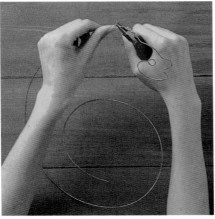

10 To make the dolphin, cut a 108 cm
(42½ in) length of 1.65 mm
(0.065 in) wire. Start at the dolphin's eye
and bend the wire around the outline to
the mouth. Bend the wire back to make a
curved line inside the body which finishes
at the tail.

11 Bind the dolphin at the mouth
and tail where the wire meets. ▶

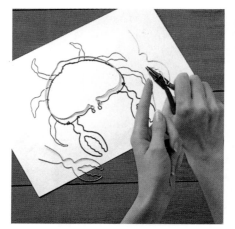

12 Form the crab's body from a 40 cm (16 in) length of 1.65 mm (0.065 in) wire. Make an eye loop at each end of the wire with round-nosed pliers. Make the front legs from two 29 cm (11½ in) lengths of 1.2 mm (0.047 in) wire.

13 Twist the ends of the legs around the wire of the crab's body and squeeze with pliers to secure.

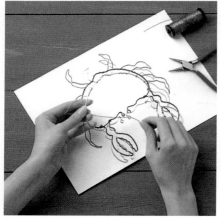

14 Use a continuous length of the thinnest wire to make the back legs, following the template. Wrap the wire around the crab's body between the legs.

15 Spray paint the sea creatures red, yellow, aquamarine, blue and green. Some of the shapes can be sprayed in two colours.

16 To assemble the mobile, attach the sea creatures to the supports with nylon thread. It is important to use the lengths of thread given so that the mobile balances. The crab hangs down 14 cm (5½ in) from the centre of the main support. The dolphin hangs 7 cm (2¾ in) and the seaweed 8 cm (3 in) from either end of one of the main supports.

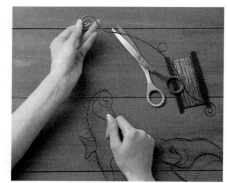

17 Hang the seahorse 11 cm (4½ in) from the end of a small support and the large fish 12 cm (4¾ in) from the other end. Tie this support so that it hangs 14 cm (5½ in) from one end of the second main support. Hang the shell 13 cm (5 in) from the other end. Hang the second small support 9 cm (3½ in) below the shell. Hang the small fish and big starfish 8 cm (3 in) from either end of the small support. Hang the small starfish 8 cm (3 in) below the large one.

CANDLE SCONCE

ESPITE ITS ORNATENESS, THIS MEDIEVAL-LOOKING CANDLE SCONCE IS QUITE EASY TO MAKE. THE BASKET CONTAINER WILL TAKE A NIGHT LIGHT OR THICK CANDLE. BY MAKING THE BASE OF THE BASKET WIDER AND WEAVING THE SIDES DEEPER YOU CAN ADAPT THE SHAPE TO FIT A LARGER CANDLE. USE SILVER-PLATED WIRE TO MAKE A LIGHTER, MORE DELICATE SCONCE TO SUIT A MORE CLASSICAL INTERIOR. ALWAYS SECURE THE CANDLE WITH CANDLE FIXES. CHECK THE DISTANCE BETWEEN THE CANDLE FLAME AND THE WALL AND DO NOT ATTACH THE SCONCE TO A WALL THAT HAS WALLPAPER OR INFLAMMABLE PAINT.

3 Bend up the wires at the edge of the circle and weave the side of the candle basket to a depth of about 2.5 cm (1 in).

1 Cut 21 38 cm (15 in) lengths of 1.65 mm (0.065 in) wire. Bundle them together so that they are even at the top and bottom, and grip them with the general-purpose pliers 16 cm (6¼ in) from one end. Hold the pliers closed with masking tape so that they act as a vice. Using the 0.8 mm (0.031 in) wire, bind around the bundle of wires for 2 cm (¾ in) from the pliers. Do not cut off the wire. Release the pliers.

2 Using round-nosed pliers, bend a downward-curving loop at the end of each wire in the bundle. Bend down the wires at right angles at the top of the bound section so that they spread out in a circle. Using the length of 0.8 mm (0.031 in) wire still attached to the bundle, weave around the wires to make a base with a diameter of 7 cm (2¾ in) (see Basic Techniques).

4 Using parallel pliers, coil down the wires to the edge of the candle basket.

MATERIALS AND EQUIPMENT YOU WILL NEED
COPPER WIRE 1.65 MM (0.065 IN) AND 0.8 MM (0.031 IN) THICK • RULER • WIRE CUTTERS • GENERAL-PURPOSE PLIERS • MASKING TAPE •
ROUND-NOSED PLIERS • PARALLEL PLIERS

5 Using parallel pliers, make two columns of coils with the wires left underneath the candle basket. Make nine coils in each column, ensuring that the second column is a mirror image of the first. Cut off the end of each wire, increasing the amount you cut off by 1 cm (½ in) each time, so that the coils decrease in size. Using round-nosed pliers, form waves in the three remaining wires. Cut off the ends of the two outer wires, so that the central one is the longest.

6 Decide which is the back of the sconce. Using the parallel pliers, unwind the two coils at the back a little, cross them over each other and twist them flat. Attach the sconce to the wall through the holes in the centre of these two coils. Bend back the wavy wires so that they support the sconce at the bottom, holding it away from the wall. Check the distance between the candle flame and the wall.

WOVEN CHAIR

YOU DON'T NEED TO HAVE DIY SKILLS TO CREATE FASHIONABLE DESIGNER FURNITURE. SECONDHAND WOODEN CHAIRS ARE CHEAP AND EASY TO FIND. BUY ONE THAT HAS A CANE OR BASKETWORK SEAT AND REMOVE IT. PAINT THE CHAIR IN ONE COLOUR AND CHOOSE WIRE OF A CONTRASTING COLOUR. THE CHAIR PICTURED HERE IS PAINTED LILAC-BLUE AND THE SEAT IS WOVEN WITH ORANGE AND BURGUNDY ENAMELLED COPPER WIRE. MAKE ONE CHAIR AS A FOCAL POINT OR A WHOLE SET FOR THE DINING ROOM. MAKE SURE THE EYELET SCREWS ARE FIRMLY SECURED AS THEY HAVE TO TAKE THE WEIGHT OF A PERSON.

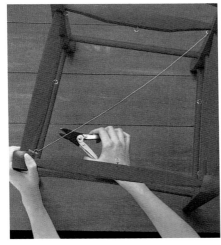

1 Screw the eyelet screws into the inside of the chair frame, one in each corner and one in the middle of each side. Secure them with pliers and make sure that the rings are lying flat.

2 Attach the 2.5 mm (0.098 in) wire to one of the corner screws by threading it through the eyelet and twisting the end around the wire, using round-nosed pliers. Stretch it diagonally across the frame and secure it to the opposite eyelet. Stretch wire across the other diagonal in the same way. Squeeze all the joins with parallel pliers.

3 Make a diamond shape between the four side screws with four more pieces of copper wire.

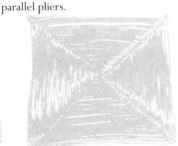

MATERIALS AND EQUIPMENT YOU WILL NEED

WOODEN CHAIR • EIGHT EYELET SCREWS • ROUND-NOSED PLIERS • ENAMELLED COPPER WIRE 2.5 MM (0.098 IN) THICK AND 1 MM (0.039 IN) THICK IN TWO COLOURS • PARALLEL PLIERS • WIRE CUTTERS

4 Cut a long length of 1 mm (0.039 in) enamelled copper wire and fold it in half. Attach it by passing the loop under the centre of the copper wire cross and threading the end back through to secure.

5 Weave a square (see Basic Techniques) until you have covered half the distance between the centre and where the copper wires cross. Cut off the wire, wrap it around several times and tuck in the end.

6 Weave four more squares, one at each point where the copper wires cross.

7 Attach another double length of 1 mm (0.039 in) enamelled copper wire to one of the corner eyelet screws.

8 Weave first around one side of the chair frame, then back around the diagonal copper wire and around the other side of the chair frame to make a herring-bone pattern.

9 Continue weaving until you reach the square nearest to that corner. Secure the wire and cut off. Weave the other three corners in the same way.

10 Loop a double length of 1 mm (0.039 in) enamelled copper wire around one of the side eyelet screws. Weave around the chair frame to one side of the eyelet, then over the eyelet, around the other side of the chair frame and back under the eyelet. Continue in this way until the eyelet is completely covered.

11 Continue weaving by wrapping the wire around the two diagonal copper wires as well as the chair frame.

12 Weave until you reach the two nearest squares. Secure the wire and cut off. Weave the other three sides in the same way.

13 Stretch two lengths of copper wire across each of the spaces between the five central woven squares. Attach the ends to the corners of the squares and secure with round-nosed pliers.

14 Using 1 mm (0.039 in) enamelled copper wire in a second colour, weave a square in each space.

15 Weave the four squares so that they are smaller than the first five and there are gaps in the finished pattern.

TOASTING FORK

TOASTING CRUMPETS OVER A REAL FIRE ON A COLD WINTER'S EVENING IS ALWAYS A PLEASANT ACTIVITY. THIS FORK IS MADE FROM FOUR WIRE COAT-HANGERS AND IS BOTH LIGHT AND STRONG. THE BOWED HANDLE AT THE TOP HELPS PREVENT THE WIRE FROM BECOMING TOO HOT. WIRE COAT-HANGERS COME IN DIFFERENT-COLOURED FINISHES, SO YOU COULD MAKE A TWO-TONE FORK, AS SHOWN IN THE BACKGROUND OF THE PICTURE. BEFORE YOU MAKE THE FORK, CHECK THAT THE FINISH ON THE COAT-HANGERS DOES NOT BURN. CUT OFF THE HOOKS AND STRAIGHTEN THE COAT-HANGERS BEFORE YOU START.

1 To make the first of the two inner struts, measure 10 cm (4 in) from the end of one of the straightened coat-hangers and wind it around a wooden spoon at this point to create a loop. The wire comes out of the loop at a slight angle. Measure 2 cm (¾ in) before bending the remaining wire straight. Make the second strut a mirror image of the first by winding the wire the other way around the wooden spoon. Make the two outer struts in the same way. This time allow 12 cm (5 in) for the prongs and bend a right angle 2 cm (¾ in) after the prong loop.

DIAGRAM 1

2 Bind the struts together temporarily with tacking wire, loosely enough to allow movement. Slide the two outer prongs through the loops of the two inner prongs, ensuring that all of the components are in the right place (see diagram 1).

3 Measure up from the prongs and mark the handle at intervals of 4 cm (1½ in), 18 cm (7 in), 4 cm (1½ in), 20 cm (8 in), 4 cm (1½ in) and 2 cm (¾ in). These measurements may vary depending on how much wire is left. Using the galvanized wire, bind the first two 4 cm (1½ in) sections. Then bind the last 4 cm (1½ in) section, but this time do not cut off the wire. Cut off three of the remaining wires at the last mark.

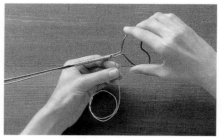

4 Make the fourth wire end into a heart shape, using pliers and bending it around a piece of copper piping to create the curves. Leave 2 cm (¾ in) at the end and bind it in with the other three wires, continuing to use the wire from the last 4 cm (1½ in) section.

5 Using the pliers, grip each wire in turn halfway along the 20 cm (8 in) section. Pull the wire so that it bows out. This will be the handle of the fork, so test it in your hand for comfort and adjust if necessary. Trim the ends of the prongs so that they are even and hammer each tip flat.

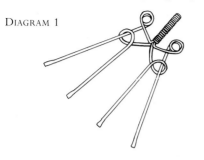

MATERIALS AND EQUIPMENT YOU WILL NEED
FOUR WIRE COAT-HANGERS • WIRE CUTTERS • RULER • WOODEN SPOON • TACKING WIRE •
PERMANENT MARKER PEN • GENERAL-PURPOSE PLIERS • GALVANIZED WIRE 0.8 MM (0.031 IN) THICK • PIECE OF COPPER PIPING • HAMMER

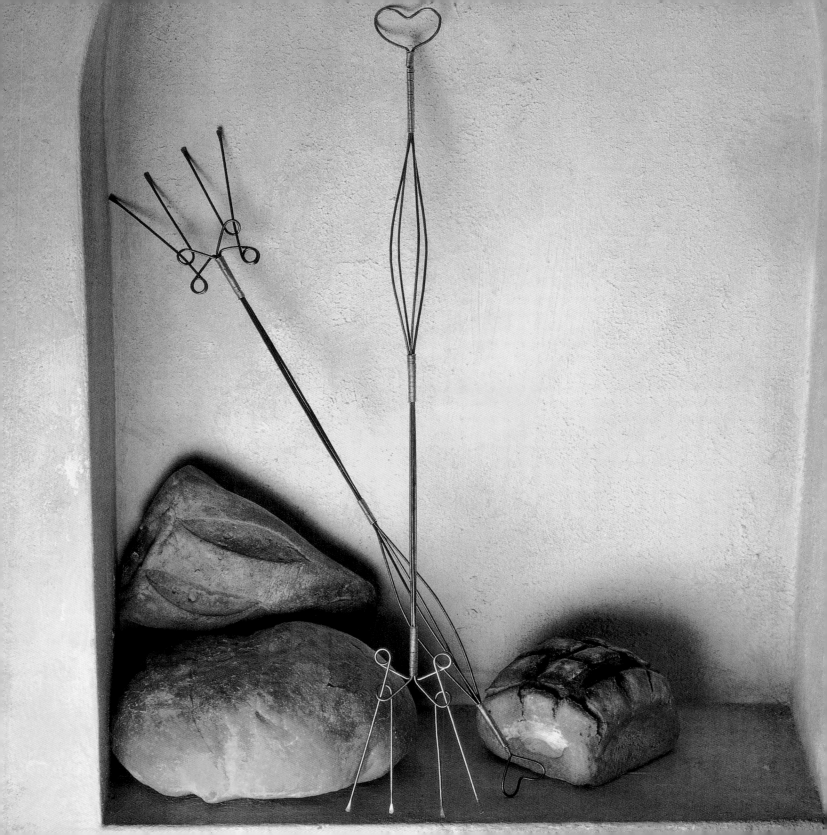

BOTTLE CARRIER

BOTTLE CARRIERS ARE EXTREMELY USEFUL BUT HARD TO FIND, SO MAKING YOUR OWN IS THE PERFECT SOLUTION. THIS CARRIER IS MADE FROM THICK GALVANIZED WIRE AND HOLDS THREE BOTTLES. BY ADDING THREE MORE CORE WIRES, YOU CAN ADD ANOTHER LEAF TO THE CLOVER SHAPE TO HOLD FOUR BOTTLES. IN THE PAST, FRENCH WIRE WINE BOTTLE CARRIERS OFTEN INCLUDED A CANDLE HOLDER, MAKING THEM ESPECIALLY USEFUL FOR FETCHING BOTTLES FROM DARK WINE CELLARS. THESE CARRIERS ARE NOW QUITE RARE HARD TO FIND AS THEY ARE MUCH SOUGHT AFTER BY COLLECTORS.

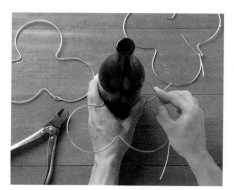

1 Cut three 80 cm (32 in) lengths of 2 mm (0.078 in) wire. Leave a 10 cm (4 in) allowance at the end of each wire and bend the wire at this point. Wrap the next section of wire around a bottle and bend back the wire where it meets the first bend. Make two more petals in this way. The circles will spring open to make the clover shape. Make a loop at each end of the wire and close together. Cut off any excess wire. Make two more clover shapes.

2 Cut seven 80 cm (32 in) and two 90 cm (36 in) lengths of 2 mm (0.078 in) wire. Straighten all the wires and bundle them together so that the longest are in the centre and stick out at one end. This end will form the handle.

3 Starting at the point where the longer wires stick out, bind the bundle with 0.8 mm (0.031 in) wire for 42 cm (16½ in). Divide the rest of the wires into groups of three. Bend them away from the central shaft at right angles. Lay the wires in each bunch of three side by side and bind together 4.5 cm (1¾ in) from the central bend. Bind for about 2 cm (¾ in), then bend out the outer two wires at right angles. Measure 5 cm (2 in) from the bound section and mark each wire. Bend each wire up at a right angle so that it stands parallel to the handle. Make a hook at the end of each wire.

4 Slot the three clover shapes into the structure. Close up the loops around the top clover shape. Bind the bottom clover in place. Bind up each strut, securing the middle clover shape halfway up. Bind over the wire ends at the top of the structure.

5 Wrap a length of 2 mm (0.078 in) wire around the nail to make a coil. Thread the bead onto the wires at the top of the central shaft. Apply strong glue to the coil and hammer it into the bead.

MATERIALS AND EQUIPMENT YOU WILL NEED

GALVANIZED GARDEN WIRE 2 MM (0.078 IN) AND 0.8 MM (0.031 IN) THICK • RULER • WIRE CUTTERS • GENERAL-PURPOSE PLIERS • BOTTLE • 4 MM (³⁄₁₆ IN NAIL) • LARGE WOODEN BEAD • STRONG GLUE • HAMMER

BICYCLE TOY

An African toy was the inspiration for this project. Handmade from wire and scrap materials, it was ingeniously designed so that a little figure pedalled a bicycle when the toy was pushed along. This bicycle toy and the toys pictured in the History of Wire on the same mechanical principle. You could adapt the figure to your liking by your choice of accessories, such as the bicycle basket, the fabrics used for the clothes and the colours of the pipe cleaners. A second toy can be dressed as a boy to make a pair.

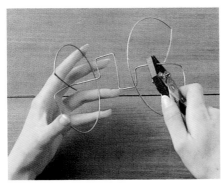

1 To make the bicycle, cut a 1 m (40 in) length of galvanized wire. Using permanent marker pen, mark the wire at intervals of 5 cm (2 in), 31 cm (12¼ in), 5 cm (2 in), 3 cm (1¼ in), 2 cm (¾ in), 2 cm (¾ in), 4 cm (1½ in), 2 cm (¾ in), 2 cm (¾ in), 3 cm (1¼ in), 5 cm (2 in), 31 cm (12¼ in) and 5 cm (2 in). Wrap both 31 cm (12¼ in) sections of wire around a bottle or can with a diameter of approximately 10 cm (4 in) to form the wheels. Using parallel pliers, bend in the 5 cm (2 in) at each end of the wire to form a radius to the centre of the circle.

2 Bend in the other two 5 cm (2 in) sections at right angles. Make the bicycle pedals by bending right angles in the wire at the marked points.

3 Bend each wheel so that it is at a right angle to the pedals.

4 Transfer the twisty wire tape to a cotton reel to make it easier to handle. Bind tape around the wheel, along the radius, across the pedals and round the second wheel.

▶

MATERIALS AND EQUIPMENT YOU WILL NEED

GALVANIZED WIRE 1.65 MM (0.065 IN) THICK • RULER • WIRE CUTTERS • PERMANENT MARKER PENS • BOTTLE OR CAN • PARALLEL PLIERS • TWISTY WIRE TAPE IN TWO COLOURS • COTTON REEL • COLOURED PIPE CLEANERS • SWEET TUBE • PAPER FASTENERS • SELECTION OF LARGE AND SMALL WOODEN BEADS • STRONG GLUE • RIBBON • DOLL'S STRAW HAT • FABRIC IN TWO COLOURS • NEEDLE AND THREAD • DOUBLE-SIDED STICKY TAPE • FREEZER BAG TIES • DOLL'S BASKET • SILK FLOWERS • GREEN BAMBOO CANE

DIAGRAM 1

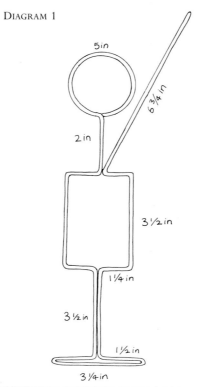

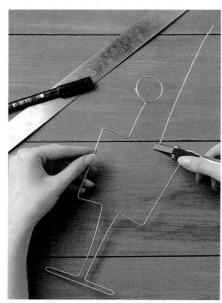

5 To make the body of the bicycle, cut a 1 m (40 in) length of galvanized wire and mark it at intervals of 12 cm (5 in), 5 cm (2 in), 3 cm (1¼ in), 9 cm (3½ in), 3 cm (1¼ in), 9 cm (3½ in), 4 cm (1½ in), 8.5 cm (3¼ in), 4 cm (1½ in), 9 cm (3½ in), 3 cm (1¼ in), 9 cm (3½ in), 3 cm (1¼ in) and 17 cm (6¾ in). Cut off any excess and follow diagram 1 to shape the bicycle. Use parallel pliers to bend right angles at the marked points. Bend the 12 cm (5 in) section into a circle to form the seat. Leave the 17 cm (6¾ in) section at the other end to be inserted into the bamboo cane later.

6 Bend up the handlebars, seat and stick attachment at right angles.

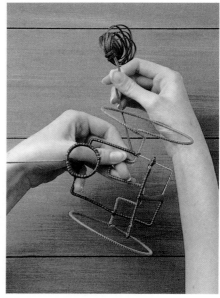

7 Bind twisty wire tape in another colour around the handlebars, leaving a tiny gap near each end where you will attach the doll's hands. Bind down the neck of the handlebars and along the frame. Halfway along the frame, bind the body onto one side of the wheels. Bind the seat, leaving the projecting wire bare. Continue binding around the frame, binding on the wheels at the other side. The wheels should now rotate when you push the bike along gently.

8 To make the doll's body, twist together the ends of two pipe cleaners. Make a hole either side of the top and bottom of the tube. Thread the joined pipe cleaners through the holes at the top to make the arms. To make the upper legs, bend two pipe cleaners in half and twist the ends together. Attach each pipe cleaner to one of the holes at the bottom of the tube with a paper fastener. Do not fasten them too tightly as they must allow for movement.

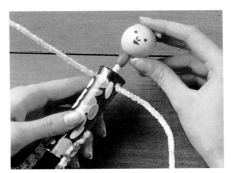

9 Draw a face in permanent marker pen on a large, plain bead. Make a hole in the end of the tube. Thread a pipe cleaner through the hole. Thread on a small bead for the neck and then the large bead. Bend the pipe cleaner over the top of the head and over the bottom edge of the tube so that the head is held on securely.

10 Bend two pipe cleaners in half to make the lower legs and thread through the upper legs. Wrap a brown pipe cleaner round the bottom of each leg and bend up to make the doll's shoes. Glue three brown pipe cleaners onto the top of the head and plait on each side to make the hair. Tie a ribbon onto the end of each plait. Glue on a doll's hat.

11 Cut a 10 cm (4 in) square of fabric and fray the edge. Cut a slit from one corner to the centre to make the shawl. Cut a 10 x 32 cm (4 x 13 in) rectangle from another fabric. Sew a line of running stitch along the top edge and gather to make the skirt. Wrap a piece of strong double-sided sticky tape around the doll's body. Dress the doll and tie a ribbon around the waist.

12 Attach the doll's feet to the pedals with freezer bag ties. Wrap each arm around the handlebars, twisting the excess length around the arm. Place a little basket over one arm first and fill it with silk flowers.

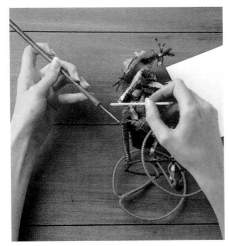

13 Apply strong glue to the piece of wire projecting from the bicycle seat and insert into the hollow centre of a green bamboo cane. Allow the glue to dry. Apply glue to the top end of the cane and slide on two or three beads to make a handle. Toddler's beads are best for this as they have large holes.

COPPER BOWL

COPPER WIRE IS NATURALLY WARM IN COLOUR AND THE WRAPPING TECHNIQUE USED HERE ENHANCES ITS RICH APPEARANCE. THE BOWL LOOKS PARTICULARLY SOFT AND SUMPTUOUS WHEN DISPLAYED BY CANDLELIGHT. THE ORGANIC LOOK OF THE COILED TENDRILS MAKES THE BOWL SUITABLE FOR HOLDING FRUIT. FOR A SPECIAL DINNER PARTY, MAKE MATCHING NAPKIN RINGS FROM 60 CM (24 IN) LENGTHS OF WRAPPED WIRE. MAKE A CYLINDRICAL COIL IN THE MIDDLE TO HOLD THE NAPKIN AND A FLAT COIL AT EACH END. COPPER TARNISHES, SO POLISH IT REGULARLY TO KEEP IT SHINY.

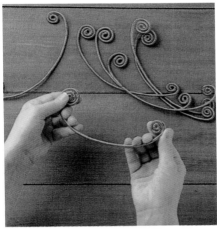

4 Bend the longer wrapped wire around the larger bowl and the shorter wire around the smaller bowl to make two wire hoops.

1 Cut eight 42 cm (16½ in) lengths of the 2 mm (0.078 in) copper wire. Wrap them with 0.8 mm (0.031 in) wire (see Basic Techniques). Make a coil with a diameter of about 3.5 cm (1½ in) at one end of each wire and one of 2.5 cm (1 in) at the other, using parallel pliers.

2 Using your hands, bend each wire to form the curved side struts of the bowl. Use the first one as a model for the rest so that they all have the same shape.

3 To make the top and bottom rims of the bowl, cut two lengths of 2.65 mm (0.104 in) wire, one 80 cm (32 in) and the other 50 cm (20 in). Wrap the longer length in 1.2 mm (0.047 in) wire and the shorter in 1.5 mm (0.059 in) wire. Pull each wire out from its coil by 2 cm (¾ in). This will create a short projecting wire at one end and a length of empty coil at the other.

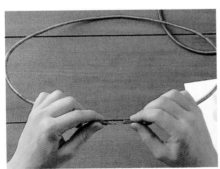

5 Insert a little quick-drying glue into the empty end of each coil and slot in the projecting end of wire. Hold it firmly in place until the glue is dry.

▶

MATERIALS AND EQUIPMENT YOU WILL NEED

COPPER WIRE 2.65 MM (0.104 IN), 2 MM (0.078 IN), 1.5 MM (0.059 IN), 1.2 MM (0.047 IN), 1 MM (0.039 IN) AND 0.8 MM (0.031 IN) THICK • RULER • WIRE CUTTERS • PARALLEL PLIERS • BOWLS IN TWO SIZES • QUICK-DRYING GLUE • PERMANENT MARKER PEN • GENERAL-PURPOSE PLIERS

6 Lightly mark eight equidistant points around each hoop. Cut 16 12 cm (5 in) lengths of 1 mm (0.039 in) wire. Use these wires to begin binding the side struts to the hoops. Allow the struts to extend above the top rim by 6 cm (2½ in) and below the bottom rim by 4 cm (1½ in).

7 Continue to bind the struts to the hoops, wiring alternate ones first. This helps to give the bowl stability as you work, although it will be a bit wobbly at this stage.

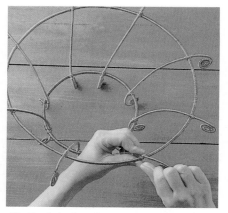

8 Bind the last four struts to the hoops, adjusting any that become misshapen in the process.

9 Make an open coil (see Basic Techniques) with a diameter of 15 cm (6 in) from 2.65 mm (0.104 in) copper wire. Bind the spiral in place with two lengths of 1 mm (0.039 in) copper wire, leaving 10 cm (4 in) spare at each end.

10 Attach the base coil to the bottom rim by binding the excess wire around four of the struts.

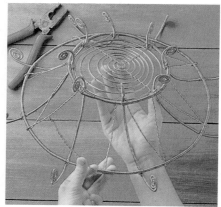

11 Twist a 2.5 m (2½ yd) double length of 1 mm (0.039 in) copper wire and wrap it around the bowl (see Basic Techniques). Make a zigzag pattern between the struts at the bottom and halfway between the struts around the top rim.

ANGEL

ONCE YOU HAVE BECOME DEXTROUS AT SCULPTING WIRE, TRY MAKING THIS ELEGANT CHRISTMAS ANGEL. THE SILVER-PLATED COPPER WIRE IS SOFT AND EASY TO BEND. THE ANGEL MAKES A NOVEL ADVENT CALENDAR. HANG A DIFFERENT ORNAMENT, SUCH AS A BEAD, A STAR OR A SMALL BAUBLE, FROM HER HAND EVERY DAY. ON CHRISTMAS DAY, HANG A LITTLE PRESENT TO BE OPENED. THE ANGEL CAN ALSO BE HUNG ON THE TREE OR IN THE CENTRE OF A WREATH. YOU COULD CREATE OTHER WIRE DECORATIONS FOR THE TREE. DRAW OR TRACE CHRISTMAS MOTIFS AS TEMPLATES TO SCULPT AROUND.

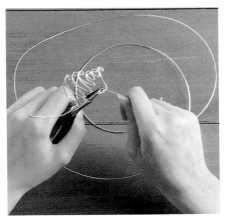

1 The template of the Angel appears on page 93. Use this as a guide for shaping the wire. You can either use it the same size or enlarge it using a photocopier. Then, leaving 5 cm (2 in) at the end start bending the wire around the template, using round-nosed pliers and your fingers. Make the hair curls and the forehead up to the eye. Make the lower lid of the eye first and then the upper lid. Halfway along the upper lid, make a loop around the end of the round-nosed pliers to form the pupil. Squeeze the corner of the eye with parallel pliers.

2 Shape the nose and make a slightly larger loop around the end of the round-nosed pliers for the nostril. Shape the mouth, closing the lips with the parallel pliers, and then shape the chin.

3 Loop the wire around the bottom of the hair to make the cheek. This loop will help to keep the structure flat and more manageable.

4 Follow the template along the arm. Make loops with the round-nosed pliers for the fingers and shape the bottom line of the arm.

5 Make the shoulder by looping the wire carefully around the point where the arm joins the neck. ▶

MATERIALS AND EQUIPMENT YOU WILL NEED

PHOTOCOPIER AND PAPER • SILVER- OR GOLD-PLATED WIRE 1 MM (0.039 IN) THICK • ROUND-NOSED PLIERS • PARALLEL PLIERS • WIRE CUTTERS •
NARROW RIBBON • STAR-SHAPED BEAD OR CRYSTAL DROPLET

6 At the waist, bend the wire across to form the waistband. Make a series of long horizontal loops with slightly curled ends back along the waistband. When you have made seven loops, secure with a tight twist at the bend.

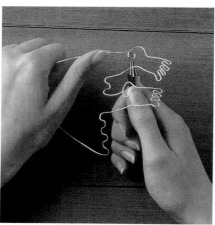

7 Make a large curve for the lower part of the skirt. Shape a wavy hem around the thickest part of the round-nosed pliers. The legs interrupt the wavy hemline. Make the toes in the same way as the fingers, only they should be shorter and rounder. Shape the heel and make a loop at the ankle.

8 Complete the wavy hemline and the back of the skirt. Secure by twisting the wire tightly around the waistband.

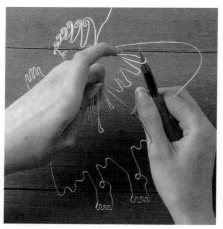

9 Make loops along the bottom of the wing and close slightly to neaten. Form the curved top of the wing.

10 Loop the wire around the back of the shoulder and under the bottom of the wing. Finish off with a coil and cut off the wire.

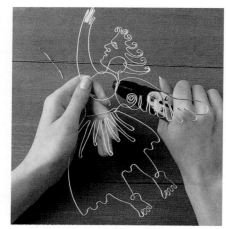

11 Using the 5 cm (2 in) of wire left at the start, bind the shoulder and wing together. Cut off the end. Thread ribbon through the loops in the waistband and hang a star-shaped bead or crystal droplet from the angel's hand.

WOVEN BOTTLE

HERE'S AN UNUSUAL WAY OF RECYCLING THOSE BEAUTIFUL BOTTLES THAT ARE TOO NICE TO THROW AWAY. THE WOVEN WIRE CASING IS NOT ONLY DECORATIVE BUT ALSO PROTECTS THE BOTTLE FROM BREAKAGE. ALTHOUGH THE TECHNIQUE IS LABOUR-INTENSIVE AND REQUIRES PATIENCE, IT IS RELATIVELY EASY TO MASTER. THE FINISHED BOTTLE CAN BE USED AS A VASE, DECANTER OR CANDLE HOLDER, BUT USE NON-DRIP CANDLES. TO DISPLAY THE BOTTLE TO ITS BEST ADVANTAGE, PLACE IT IN A POSITION WHERE THE LIGHT WILL SHINE THROUGH AND REVEAL THE COLOUR OF THE GLASS WITHIN. YOU COULD MAKE A SET OF BOTTLES OF VARYING SIZES, SHAPES AND COLOURS, ALSO USING DIFFERENT COLOURS OF WIRE.

1 Cut four pieces of 1.65 mm (0.065 in) wire 24 cm (10 in) longer than twice the height of the bottle. Cross the wires on the base of the bottle (you can see this in step two) and bend so that eight struts run up the sides of the bottle. Tuck the wire ends inside the neck and wrap masking tape around the body and neck of the bottle.

2 Join a doubled length of the thin wire to the point where the wires cross and start weaving (see Basic Techniques).

3 Loop the wire around each strut, creating a smooth, closely woven surface. Change the wire every so often to achieve a stripy pattern.

4 Continue weaving around the sides of the bottle, twisting the wires together where you join them.

5 When you have woven to the top of the bottle, pull out the ends of the wire struts from inside the bottle. Using round-nosed pliers, make downward-curving coils.

6 Continue to weave fine enamelled copper wire around the coils. You will now see the reverse pattern of the weave. Secure the last end of wire by wrapping it several times around a strut before cutting off.

MATERIALS AND EQUIPMENT YOU WILL NEED
BOTTLE • ENAMELLED COPPER WIRE 1.65 MM (0.065 IN) THICK AND 0.65 MM (0.025 IN) THICK IN TWO COLOURS • RULER • WIRE CUTTERS • MASKING TAPE • ROUND-NOSED PLIERS

TOAST RACK

GRACE YOUR BREAKFAST TABLE WITH THIS SCULPTURAL TOAST RACK. THE TIGHT WIRE WRAPPING AND STAR PATTERNS ON THE HANDLE AND FEET BEADS GIVE THE PIECE AN ORIGINAL SPACE AGE QUALITY. THE SPRINGY, ELONGATED ARCHES ARE SPACED TO ALLOW FOR THICK OR THIN SLICES OF BREAD. CHOOSE BEADS WITH QUITE LARGE HOLES OR ENLARGE THEM BY DRILLING TO FIT THE STRUCTURAL WIRE. MATCHING EGG CUPS CAN BE MADE BY COILING WRAPPED WIRE AROUND AN EGG THEN NARROWING IT TO MAKE A NECK AND WIDENING IT AGAIN TO MAKE A BASE.

1 Cut a 10 cm (4 in) length of 2.65 mm (0.104 in) wire and use round-nosed pliers to bend a loop in one end to make a "key". Attach the 1.2 mm (0.047 in) copper wire next to the loop and wrap for 2 cm (¾ in). Do not cut the wire off.

2 Cut two 24 cm (10 in) lengths of 2.65 mm (0.104 in) copper wire for the main shafts. Place the key at a right angle to one of the 24 cm (10 in) lengths of wire, 1 cm (½ in) from the end. Wrap the shaft with the same length of 1.2 mm (0.047 in) wire for 22 cm (9 in) by turning the key.

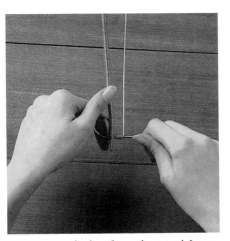

3 Remove the key from the initial 2 cm (¾ in) of wrapping and place at a right angle to the other end of the 24 cm (10 in) piece of wire. Wrap the key for another 2 cm (¾ in), making sure that this coil sticks out from the shaft wire at the same side as the first. Cut off the wrapping wire.

▶

MATERIALS AND EQUIPMENT YOU WILL NEED
COPPER WIRE 2.65 MM (0.104 IN) AND 1.2 MM (0.047 IN) THICK • RULER • WIRE CUTTERS • ROUND-NOSED PLIERS • TACKING WIRE • BOTTLE • FILE • PERMANENT MARKER PEN • STRONG GLUE • SILVER-PLATED COPPER WIRE 0.8 MM (0.031 IN THICK) • FOUR MEDIUM-SIZED BEADS • LARGE BEAD • DRILL (OPTIONAL)

4 Remove the key from the coil and trim off the shaft wire close to the coil at each end. Wrap the second shaft wire in exactly the same way. Cut two 35 cm (13¾ in) lengths of 2.65 mm (0.104 in) wire. Wrap these two wires in the same way as the first two, this time leaving 7 cm (2¾ in) unwrapped wire at each end. Do not cut off the unwrapped sections as these will form the legs later.

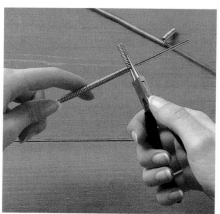

5 Using round-nosed pliers, adjust all the 2 cm (¾ in) coils so that they stick out from the wrapped wires at right angles and point in the same direction.

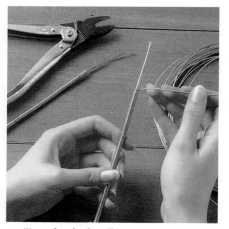

6 To make the handle struts, cut two 21 cm (8¼ in) lengths of 2.65 mm (0.104 in) wire. Make a 2 cm (¾ in) coil on the key as before, then begin wrapping one of the wires 1 cm (½ in) from the end. Wrap for 14 cm (5½ in), and cut off the wrapping wire, leaving a long end. Wrap the second handle strut in the same way but do not cut off the wrapping wire.

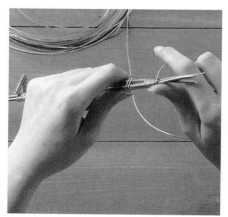

7 Tack the two handle struts together using tacking wire, checking that the coils are facing in the same direction. Wrap them together, continuing up from the 14 cm (5½ in) wrapped sections. Leave 2 cm (¾ in) at the top unwrapped.

8 To make the base, cut a 50 cm (20 in) length of 2.65 mm (0.104 in) wire. Leave 15 cm (6 in) at one end and bend the next section around a small bottle 6-7 cm (2½-2¾ in) in diameter. Wrap another length of 2.65 mm (0.104 in) wire for 13 cm (5 in) and cut off the wrapping wire. Remove the length of wire and thread the 13 cm (5 in) coil onto the bent wire. Move it along the wire until it sits in the bend.

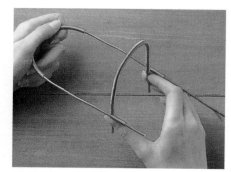

9 Bend each of the four wrapped pieces to make a curve in the centre. Thread the first wrapped section onto the base. It should be one of the pieces with 7 cm (2¾ in) legs. If you have difficulty pushing the wires through the coils, file the ends of the base wire. Pull apart the individually wrapped struts of the handle section and bend them to make an arch shape.

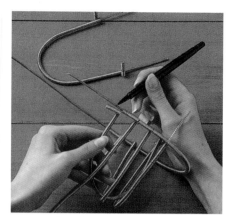

10 Thread on the next piece (with no legs), followed by the handle arch. Before threading on the next piece, mark the base wire halfway along the length of the next coil. You will cut the wire at this point later. Thread on this piece, followed by the second piece with legs. Wrap a length of 2.65 mm (0.104 in) wire for 9 cm (3½ in) and remove the coil.

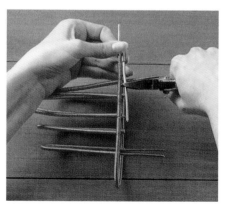

11 Thread the 9 cm (3½ in) coil onto the long end of the base wire. Bend the wire around the bottle to mirror the first curve and until the two wrapped sections meet. Cut off the wire where it meets the marked point on the base wire. Remove the last two coils from this side of the base wire and cut off at the marked point.

12 Thread the first coil onto the base wire next to the curve. Apply some strong glue to the end of the base wire and slot it into the empty section of the next coil. Allow the glue to dry.

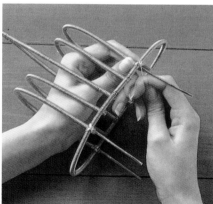

13 Using silver-plated copper wire, bind crosses around the leg joints to add stability. If you find that the rack is too springy, carefully apply a little glue to the joints.

14 Make four 5 cm (2 in) coils of 1.2 mm (0.047 in) wire by wrapping around a length of 2.65 mm (0.104 in) wire and then removing. Thread these coils onto the legs and glue on bead feet. Glue the large bead onto the top of the handle. If necessary, make the hole in the bead larger by drilling.

LANTERN

CHICKEN WIRE BECOMES AN EXOTIC MATERIAL WHEN USED TO MAKE THIS LANTERN, WHICH IS PERFECT FOR HANGING IN THE GARDEN. FOR AN EVENING GARDEN PARTY, MAKE SEVERAL IN DIFFERENT SHAPES AND SIZES AND HANG THEM AROUND THE GARDEN TO CREATE A MAGICAL ATMOSPHERE. PLACE LONG-LASTING NIGHT LIGHTS IN THE JAM JARS. THE JARS PROTECT THE CANDLE FLAME FROM THE BREEZE AND FROM FALLING LEAVES. DESPITE THE HOMELY MATERIALS, THE LANTERN ALSO LOOKS VERY EFFECTIVE WHEN HUNG INDOORS. WEAR GLOVES WHEN WORKING WITH CHICKEN WIRE TO PROTECT YOUR HANDS.

1 Cut two pieces of chicken wire, 18 x 60 cm (7 x 24 in) and 22 x 55 cm (8½ x 21½ in), and two lengths of galvanized wire, one 65 cm (26 in), the other 60 cm (24 in). Form two cylinders from the chicken wire and join the short edges together with aluminium wire (see Basic Techniques). Bend the galvanized wire to form two hoops with the same circumference as the cylinders. Bind the ends together with aluminium wire.

2 Use the aluminium wire to bind a hoop onto the edge of each cylinder.

3 To shape the lantern, which is the larger cylinder, bend all the holes in the chicken wire into heart shapes (see Basic Techniques). Use round-nosed pliers and your hands to mould the cylinder (see step eight for shape).

4 To make the lid, bend all the holes in the second cylinder into heart shapes, then push the wire to form a curved lid shape. You will need to squash the holes together at the top.

5 Using the hollow section in the mouth of the general-purpose pliers, carefully crimp the chicken wire in the centre of each section to form a central core (see Basic Techniques).

▶

MATERIALS AND EQUIPMENT YOU WILL NEED

SMALL-GAUGE CHICKEN WIRE • GALVANIZED WIRE 1.65 MM (0.065 IN) THICK • RULER • WIRE CUTTERS • GLOVES • ALUMINIUM WIRE 1 MM (0.039 IN) THICK • ROUND-NOSED PLIERS • GENERAL-PURPOSE PLIERS • BOTTLE WITH CONE-SHAPED LID • JAM JAR • LARGE BEADS • BATH PLUG CHAIN • METAL RING • FLAT-HEADED JEWELLERY PINS • THIN RIBBON (OPTIONAL)

6 To form a long cone to go on the lid of the lantern, wrap the aluminium wire around the tapered top of a paint or glue bottle. The bottom of the cone must be wide enough to fit over the central core of the lid.

7 Secure a length of thin wire inside the centre of the lid and push it through the core. Thread the coiled cone onto the wire and slip over the core. Leave the length of wire hanging loose from the centre of the cone. Wrap another length of wire around the core of the lantern section to make a smaller coil.

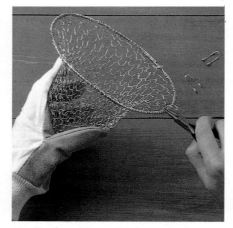

8 Cut four 10 cm (4 in) pieces of galvanized wire. Using round-nosed pliers, bend each piece into a loop with a hook at each end. Curve up the bend in each loop slightly. Position the loops evenly around the rim of the lantern section and close up the hooks with pliers.

9 Cut two lengths of galvanized wire and twist together around the neck of the jam jar so that the ends stick out on either side. Attach the wires to the rim of the lantern on either side of two opposite

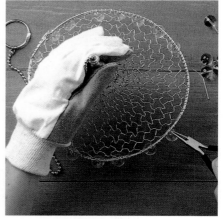

10 Thread a large metallic bead onto the wire left loose in the centre of the lid. Bind the bath plug chain to the wire and cut off the excess wire. Attach the ring to the other end of the chain for hanging. Thread beads onto flat-headed jewellery pins and hang evenly around the rim of the lid. Attach another large bead to the core of the lantern section.

11 Put the lid on the lantern and slot the four loops on the lantern rim through the chicken wire of the lid. Press them down firmly. It is very important for safety that the loops hold the bottom securely in place. Reinforce with extra pieces of wire or tie with thin ribbon.

SPICE RACK

KEEP YOUR HERB AND SPICE JARS TIDY IN THIS HEART-RIMMED RACK, WHICH IS DESIGNED TO HOLD FIVE STANDARD-SIZED SPICE JARS. IT CAN BE HUNG ON THE WALL OR USED FREE-STANDING ON A SHELF OR KITCHEN SURFACE. SCALE UP THE DESIGN AND USE THICKER WIRE TO MAKE A DISTINCTIVE WINDOW BOX. USE IT TO HOLD POT PLANTS OR LINE IT WITH MOSS, FILL WITH EARTH AND PLANT. IF YOU DO CHOOSE TO MAKE THE ENLARGED VERSION, MAKE SURE YOUR WORKING SPACE IS LARGE ENOUGH TO TWIST THE LONG LENGTHS OF WIRE THAT YOU WILL NEED (SEE BASIC TECHNIQUES).

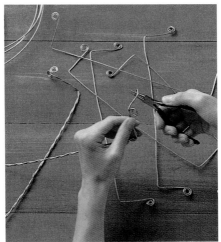

1 Cut five 45 cm (18 in) lengths of 1.65 mm (0.065 in) galvanized wire. Using permanent marker pen, mark the wire at intervals of 5 cm (2 in), 5 cm (2 in), 25 cm (10 in), 5 cm (2 in) and 5 cm (2 in). Using round-nosed pliers, bend the 5 cm (2 in) sections at the ends of each wire into coils. Using general-purpose pliers, bend up each wire at right angles at the next 5 cm (2 in) marks. Twist a length of wire then cut two 45 cm (18 in) lengths and mark in the same way. Unravel the 5 cm (2 in) at either end of each wire and make four coils, two at each end, then bend right angles at the next marks.

2 Cut two 9 cm (3½ in) lengths of 1.65 mm (0.065 in) galvanized wire. Make the box section of the spice rack by joining together the two twisted wire struts. Twist the ends of the 9 cm (3½ in) lengths around the bent corners of the struts, leaving a distance of 6 cm (2½ in) between the two struts.

3 Cut a 101 cm (41 in) length of twisted wire and mark it at intervals of 20 cm (8 in), 12 cm (5 in), 6 cm (2½ in), 25 cm (10 in), 6 cm (2½ in), 12 cm (5 in) and 20 cm (8 in). Bend a right angle at each marked point to form a rectangle. Using your hands, bend the 20 cm (8 in) section at each end of the wire to form the two halves of a heart shape. ▶

MATERIALS AND EQUIPMENT YOU WILL NEED
GALVANIZED WIRE 1.65 MM (0.065 IN) AND 0.65 MM (0.025 IN) THICK • RULER • WIRE CUTTERS • PERMANENT MARKER PEN
• ROUND-NOSED PLIERS • GENERAL-PURPOSE PLIERS • GALVANIZED WIRE 1.65 MM (0.065 IN) THICK, PREVIOUSLY DOUBLED AND TWISTED
(SEE BASIC TECHNIQUES) • TACKING WIRE • BROOMSTICK

4 Attach the four corners of the heart rim to the top of the box section using tacking wire.

5 Cut four 54 cm (21½ in) lengths of twisted wire and mark each at intervals of 5 cm (2 in), 5 cm (2 in), 6 cm (2½ in) and 38 cm (15 in). Unravel the 5 cm (2 in) end of each wire and make into two coils. Bend each wire at right angles at the next two marked points. Bend each 38 cm (15 in) section into a coil. Bend a curve in the wire next to two of the coils so they will rest on the back.

6 Slot the box section inside these four pieces so that the four large coils are at the back beside the heart. Tack into place where the pieces touch.

7 Slot the plain wire struts made in step one inside the box structure. Space evenly across the width of the box and tack into place.

8 Wrap a long length of 1.65 mm (0.065 in) wire several times around a broomstick to make a loose coil. Position this wire coil inside the front edge of the spice rack.

9 Using 0.65 mm (0.025 in) galvanized wire, bind around the top rim of the box (see Basic Techniques), securing each piece in position and removing the tacking wire as you go. Then bind from front to back along the bottom struts. Finish by binding the heart closed at the top and bottom, and binding the decorative spirals where they touch.

HOOK RACK

A RACK OF HOOKS IS ALWAYS USEFUL, AND CAN BE HUNG IN THE HALL FOR KEYS, IN THE BATHROOM FOR TOWELS AND IN THE KITCHEN FOR UTENSILS. DURING THE NINETEENTH CENTURY, MANY TYPES OF WIRE WALL RACKS WERE MADE. THE FLATTENED COIL WAS A POPULAR DECORATIVE DEVICE, AS WAS THE CLOVER MOTIF. THE BINDING TECHNIQUE ON THE STEMS IS USEFUL TO LEARN FOR OTHER PROJECTS, SUCH AS THE TOASTING FORK AND EGG TREE. THIS IS A GOOD PROJECT TO WITH MAKE CHILDREN, AS IT IS QUITE STRAIGHT-FORWARD AND THE PLASTIC-COATED WIRE IS SAFE TO USE.

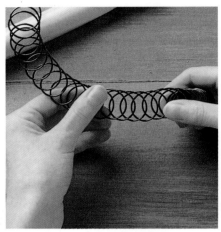

1 Tightly wrap the garden wire 40 times around a broomstick. Leave 10 cm (4 in) of wire spare at each end and cut off. Flatten the coil (see Basic Techniques). The coil should be about 30 cm (12 in) long.

2 Cut a 56 cm (22 in) length of garden wire. Mark the centre point and the point 15 cm (6 in) from each end. Form a loop at each point by wrapping the wire around a pencil. Thread the wire through the flattened coil. Slot the loop at either end of the coil into the small end loops on the wire.

3 Bend the 15 cm (6 in) section at each end of the wire around a wooden spoon to create three clover leaves. There should be about 2 cm (¾ in) left at the end to bend back down the stem. Use the 10 cm (4 in) of wire left at the ends of the coil to bind the stem.

MATERIALS AND EQUIPMENT YOU WILL NEED

GREEN GARDEN WIRE • BROOMSTICK • RULER • WIRE CUTTERS • PERMANENT MARKER PEN • PENCIL • WOODEN SPOON •
ROUND-NOSED PLIERS • A FRIEND

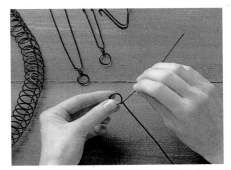

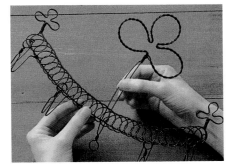

6 Slot the clover hook through the middle of the coil, so that its shank lies either side of the central loop in the bottom wire. Bend up the hook 5 cm (2 in) from the circle end. Screw the rack to the wall through the three loops in the bottom wire. The central screw will hold the hook firmly in place.

4 Cut four 30 cm (12 in) lengths of wire. Loosely bend each wire in half and wrap the bend around a spoon to make a circle. Twist the circle closed. Bend small hooks in the ends of the wires. Bend each wire in half to form four large hooks. Loop the ends of the hooks around the coil and bottom wire of the frame and close tightly.

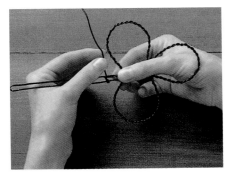

5 Cut a 2 m (79 in) length of wire. Loosely bend it in half and wrap the bend around a wooden spoon to make a circle. Twist the circle closed. Mark the point 15 cm (6 in) up from the circle and ask a friend to hold this point firmly while you twist the wires together. Bend the twisted wire around the broomstick to make three clover leaves, then bind the shape closed.

EGG TREE

THE DESIGN FOR THIS WHIMSICAL EGG TREE DERIVES FROM EASTERN European FOLK ART. THE BASKET AT THE BOTTOM IS TRADITIONALLY USED FOR BREAD. THE TREE MAKES A SPECTACULAR CENTREPIECE AT EASTER WHEN FILLED WITH DYED OR PAINTED EGGS. AT CHRISTMAS, TURN IT INTO A DECORATIVE CHRISTMAS TREE BY PUTTING NIGHT LIGHTS IN THE EGG HOLDERS AND FILLING THE BASKET WITH PRESENTS OR SWEETS. TINNED COPPER WIRE HAS BEEN USED HERE AS IT IS IDEAL FOR KITCHENWARE. IT IS AS MALLEABLE AS COPPER WIRE AND HAS THE ADDED ADVANTAGE THAT IT DOES NOT TARNISH. THE EGG TREE CAN OF COURSE BE MADE FROM CHEAPER AND MORE READILY AVAILABLE WIRE. FOR A DIFFERENT FINISH IT COULD BE WRAPPED IN NATURAL-COLOURED STRING.

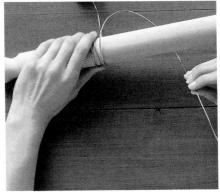

1 Measure 60 cm (24 in) of 2 mm (0.078 in) tinned copper wire but do not cut off. Mark the point and wrap this section of wire three times around a rolling pin. Remove from the rolling pin and grip the middle of the final loop between your thumb and forefinger. Wrap the loop around your thumb and pull it down. The second loop should now be reduced in diameter. These three loops form the egg holder. Refine the shape by moulding it around a large egg.

2 Bend the remaining end of wire up the outside of the egg holder to meet the wire still attached to the spool.

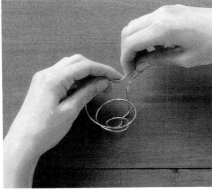

3 Bend both wires away from the egg holder to make the branch.

4 Bind the two branch wires together using 8 cm (3 in) of 1 mm (0.039 in) wire. Bend the wires down at a right angle. Leave an allowance of 2 cm (¾ in), then cut off the end of the wire.

5 To finish off the egg holder, measure 60 cm (24 in), then cut off the wire from the spool. Make ten more egg holders in this way. The bound section of the six lower holders measures 8 cm (3 in), and the section for the five upper holders measures 4 cm (1½ in).

6 Measure 5 cm (2½ in) of 2 mm (0.078 in) wire and mark the point. Wrap the next section ten times around a pencil to form petals. Bend the petals round to form a flower. Use the first 5 cm (2½ in) of wire to join the flower together and cut off. Bend the remaining wire down from the flower at a right angle to make the stem. Cut off at 75 cm (30 in). ▶

MATERIALS AND EQUIPMENT YOU WILL NEED
TINNED COPPER WIRE 2 MM (0.078 IN) AND 1 MM (0.039 IN) THICK • RULER • PERMANENT MARKER PEN • ROLLING PIN • LARGE EGG • WIRE CUTTERS • GENERAL-PURPOSE PLIERS • PENCIL • TACKING WIRE • STRONG TAPE

7 Form the top egg holder as described in step one, but this time wrap the first loop around your thumb and pull down. Measure 70 cm (27½ in) and cut off the wire from the spool.

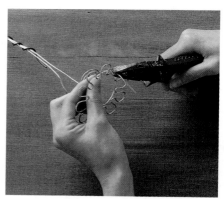

8 Bind the end of the top egg holder onto the flower opposite the join. To hold the wires in place while you are working, bind them together with tacking wire. Bend the long wire extending from the flower to curve down the outside of the spiral. Using 1 mm (0.039 in) wire, start binding the two stem wires tightly together (see Basic Techniques). Bind for 7 cm (2¾ in).

9 Bunch the stem wires of the upper five egg holders around the two stem wires to form the trunk. Wrap with a piece of strong tape to keep them in place. Using 1 mm (0.039 in) wire, start binding the trunk from just below the point where the egg holders join the stem.

10 Bind the trunk for 7 cm (2¾ in). Then bind on the six lower egg holders in the same way. Bind the trunk for approximately 25 cm (10 in) below this second tier.

11 To make the basket, cut six lengths of 2 mm (0.078 in) wire measuring 90 cm (36 in), 89 cm (35½ in), 88 cm (35 in), 75 cm (30 in), 65 cm (26 in) and 46 cm (18 in). Bend hooks at the ends of the wires and close up to make six rings. Squeeze the hooks tightly closed.

12 Splay out the wires from the base of the egg tree and curve upwards to form the side struts of the basket. Check that the diameter at the top is the same as that of the largest ring.

13 Tack the rings onto the struts, starting with the smallest at the bottom and working up to the largest at the top. Allow 2.5 cm (1 in) between each ring. Attach the largest ring by wrapping the ends of the strut wires around it. The basket should be approximately 9 cm (3½ in) in height. Bind the rings onto the struts (see Basic Techniques).

TEMPLATES

CHANDELIER

ARCHED DOUBLE COIL

← 64 mm (2½ in) →

DOUBLE COIL

SMALL GLASS HOLDER

SINGLE LOOPED COIL   NOSED DOUBLE COIL

GREETINGS CARDS

CHERUB   HEARTS

ANGEL

SEASHORE MOBILE

LARGE FISH

SHELL

CRAB

SMALL FISH

SEAHORSE

LARGE STARFISH

SEAWEED

DOLPHIN

SMALL STARFISH

SUPPLIERS

Listed here are specialist suppliers but also check in garden centres, hardware stores, craft and jewellery-making shops to see what is available.

United Kingdom

Southern Handicrafts
20 Kensington Gardens
Brighton BN1 4AL
Tel: 01273 681901
Suppliers of silver, copper and craft wire in different colours

Romany's Tools and Ironmongers
52-57 Camden High Street
London NW1 0LT
Tel: 0171 937 9570
Suppliers of light galvanized and copper wire

Buck and Ryan Ltd
101 Tottenham Court Road
London W1 0DY
Tel: 0171 636 7475
Suppliers of copper and galvanized wire

Scientific Wire Company
18 Raven Road
London E18 1HW
Tel: 0181 505 0002
Industrial suppliers of copper, tinned copper, aluminium and enamelled wire. Mail order

Australia

For most wires: BBC hardwarehouse Stores and hardware stores in every state. If fine wire is needed:

Mandrills
1 Transvaal Avenue
Double Bay NSW 2018
Tel: 2 327 7477

Twin Plaza Metals
7th Floor
227 Collins Street
Melbourne 3000
Tel: 9 654 1477

Twin Plaza Metals
250 Pitt Street
Sydney 2000
Tel: 12 264 1667

Twin Plaza Metals
55 Gawler Place
Adelaide SA 5000
Tel: 8 410 1177

Canada

Lewiscraft
2300 Yonge Street
Toronto, Ontario
M4P 1EA
Tel: 416 483 2783

Michaels – The Arts & Crafts Superstore
200 North Service Road
Oakville Town Centre 2
Oakville, Ontario
L6M 2V1
Tel: 905 842 1555

Abbey Arts & Crafts
4118 East Hastings Street
Vancouver, B.C.
Tel: 604 299 5201

ACKNOWLEDGEMENTS

The author and publishers would like to thank Andrew Gilmore, 38c Tressillian Road, London SE4 for the loo roll holder, spoon rack, toasting fork, bottle carrier, hook rack and egg tree projects; Dawn Giullas, Unit 6, Cockpit Yard, Northington Street, London WC1 for the pocket clips, greetings cards and seashore mobile projects; and Adele Tipler, 46a Balls Pond Road, London N1 for the fused flowers, woven chair and woven bottle projects.

They would also like to thank the shops that loaned wirework items for photography: Melanie Davis of Bazar, 82 Golborne Road, London W10 (0181 969 6262), page 6; Brats Ltd, 281 King's Road, London SW3 (0171 351 7674), page 8, and Stephen Goldsmith, African Fine Art and Craft, 164 Brooke Road, London E5 (0181 985 5311), page 9. The following companies kindly lent further items for photography: Robert Young Antiques, 68 Battersea Bridge Road, London SW11 (0171 228 7847); Joss Graham Oriental Textiles, London SW1 (0171 730 4370); V. V. Rouleaux, 10 Symon Street, London SW3 (0171 730 3125), and Paperchase, 213 Tottenham Court Road, London W1 (0171 580 8496).

The following artists kindly lent works of art for the gallery and would be pleased to accept commissions: Amanda Bright, Flat 14, 48 Buckingham Palace Road, Brighton BN1 3PJ; Hillary Burns, King William Cottage, Yalberton, Paignton, Devon TQ4 7PE; Susan Cross, Tel. 0131 661 3996; Paul Davis, 34a Springdale Road, Broadstone, Dorset BH18 9BU, Tel. 01202 692 687; Jane McAdam Frued, 116 Wendover, Thurlow Street, London SE17 2UE; Cathy Pilkington, Brook House, Park Lane, Poynton, Cheshire SK12 1RG; Hans Stoffler, 0181 673 2928; Rupert Till, The Annexe, Hovingham, York YO6 4LX; Adele Tipler, Tel. 0171 254 8252; Jan Truman, Wireworks, The Folly, Chewton Mendip, Bath BA3 4LE; Ester Ward, c/o Crafts Council, 44a Pentonville Road, London N1.

AUTHOR'S ACKNOWLEDGEMENTS

A special thanks to Andrew for all his help and support throughout the book, Dawn and Adele for designing and making such creative projects, Sarah and Graham for staying up all night and their literary input, and finally Captain 3D for his computer wizardry.

INDEX